The
DIRTY LIFE

On Farming, Food, and Love

KRISTIN
KIMBALL

SCRIBNER

New York   London   Toronto   Sydney

SCRIBNER
A Division of Simon & Schuster, Inc.
1230 Avenue of the Americas
New York, NY 10020

First Scribner hardcover edition October 2010

SCRIBNER and design are registered trademarks of The Gale Group, Inc.,
used under license by Simon & Schuster, Inc., the publisher of this work.

For information about special discounts for bulk purchases,
please contact Simon & Schuster Special Sales at
1-866-506-1949 or business@simonandschuster.com.

The Simon & Schuster Speakers Bureau can bring authors to your live event.
For more information or to book an event contact the Simon & Schuster Speakers Bureau
at 1-866-248-3049 or visit our website at www.simonspeakers.com.

Designed by Carla Jayne Jones

Manufactured in the United States of America

10   9   8   7   6   5   4   3   2   1

ISBN 978-1-4165-5160-7
ISBN 978-1-4391-8714-2 (ebook)

For Mom and Dad

The
DIRTY LIFE

Prologue

Saturday night, midwinter. The farmhouse has been dark for hours and the crew has all gone home. We light a fire and open two bottles of our friend Brian's homemade beer, and as I wash up the milking things Mark begins to cook for me, a farmer's expression of intimacy. He is perfectly sure of himself in the kitchen, wasting no movement, and watching him fills me with a combination of admiration and lust, like a rock star's groupie. He has chosen a fine-looking chuck steak from the side of beef we butchered this week and has brought an assembly of vegetables from the root cellar. Humming, he rummages through the fridge and comes out with a pint of rich, gelatinous chicken stock and a pomegranate, the latter a gift from my friend Amelia, who brought it up from New York City.

Mark gets busy, his hands moving quickly, and half an hour later he sets two colorful plates on the table. The steak he has broiled medium rare and sliced thin across the grain and drizzled with a red wine reduction. There is a mix of leek, carrot, and kale, sautéed in butter and seasoned with juniper berries, and next to this, vibrating with color, a tiny pile of this year's ruby sauerkraut, made from purple cabbages. We are out of bread, but he found a little ball of pastry dough in the fridge, left over from making a pie, and he rolled it out and cut it in triangles and cooked it in a hot skillet, and voilà, biscuits. But the unlikely star of the plate is the radish. Mark went a little crazy planting the storage radishes last summer and put in a thousand feet of them, a lark for which I have teased him mercilessly, but they grew so beautifully and are storing so well that now I see we might actually put a small dent in the supply by the end of the winter. The variety is called Misato Rose. Creamy white with shades of green on the outside, and bright pink on the inside, they are about the size of an apple, and, when you cut them, they look like miniature watermelons. These are a favorite appetizer served raw with a little sprinkling of salt. They look so fruitlike the biting taste is always a surprise, a disagreement between the eye and the palate. Tonight, Mark braised them in stock, which hardly dimmed their brilliant color but mellowed out their flavor. He added a dash of maple syrup and balsamic vinegar, and at the end tossed in a handful of the tangy pomegranate seeds, the heat bursting some and leaving others whole to amuse the tongue. This is why I love my husband: given these opposites to work with, the earthiest of roots and the most exotic of fruits, he sees harmony, not discord. We eat the meal, my eyes half closed in pleasure, and sip the bitter, hoppy beer, and kiss, and before my friends in the city have even dressed to go out for the evening, we slip off to bed.

I've slept in this bed for seven winters, and still, sometimes,

I wonder how I came to be here, someone's wife, in an old farmhouse in the North Country. There are still moments when I feel like an actor in a play. The real me stays out until four, wears heels, and carries a handbag, but this character I'm playing *gets up* at four, wears Carhartts, and carries a Leatherman, and the other day, doing laundry, a pair of .22 long shells fell out of her pocket, and she was supposed to act like she wasn't surprised. Instead of the lights and sounds of the city, I'm surrounded by five hundred acres that are blanketed tonight in mist and clouds, and this farm is a whole world darker and quieter, more beautiful and more brutal than I could have imagined the country to be.

Tonight, curled against Mark's body under the goose-down comforter, I hear cold spring rain begin to fall. Mark is already asleep, and I lie awake for a while, wondering if any of the cows will have the bad luck to calve in such nasty weather, if the pigs have enough straw in their hut to stay warm, if the horses are comfortable in the pasture or if they'd be better off in the barn. I worry that the rain is melting the snow cover, exposing the garlic and the perennials to the harsh cold that is sure to come back to bite them before the threat of frost is over. These are the kinds of thoughts that have occupied the majority of the human race—the agrarians—for most of the history of the world. And I am one of them now. It's as surprising to me as radishes and pomegranates.

Mark and I are both first-generation farmers. The farm we've built together could be described as antique or very modern,

depending on who you ask. The fertility comes from compos-
ted manure and tilled-in cover crops. We use no pesticides,
no herbicides. The farm is highly diversified, and most of the
work is done by horses instead of tractors. Our small fields are
bordered by hedgerow and woodlot. We have a sugar bush, the
beginnings of an orchard, an abundance of pasture and hay
ground, and perennial gardens of herbs and flowers. We milk
our cows by hand and their milk is very rich and the butter
we make from the cream is taxicab yellow. We raise hogs and
beef cattle and chickens on pasture, and at butchering time we
make fresh and dried sausages, pancetta, corned beefs, pâtés,
and quarts of velvety stock.

The food we grow feeds a hundred people. These "members" come to the farm every Friday to pick up their share of
what we've produced. Our goal is to provide everything they
need to have a healthy and satisfying diet, year-round. We supply beef, chicken, pork, eggs, milk, maple syrup, grains, flours,
dried beans, herbs, fruits, and forty different vegetables. For
this our members pay us $2,900 per person per year and can
take as much food each week as they can eat, plus extra produce, during the growing season, to freeze or can for winter.
Some members still shop regularly at the grocery store for con-
venience food, produce out of season, and things that we can't
provide like citrus fruit, but we and some of the others live
pretty much on what we produce.

I've learned many things in the years since my life took
this wild turn toward the dirt. I can shoot a gun, dispatch a
chicken, dodge a charging bull, and ride out a runaway behind
panicked horses. But one lesson came harder than any of

those: As much as you transform the land by farming, farming transforms you. It seeps into your skin along with the dirt that abides permanently in the creases of your thickened hands, the beds of your nails. It asks so much of your body that if you're not careful it can wreck you as surely as any vice by the time you're fifty, when you wake up and find yourself with ruined knees and dysfunctional shoulders, deaf from the constant clank and rattle of your machinery, and broke to boot. But farming takes root in you and crowds out other endeavors, makes them seem paltry. Your acres become a world. And maybe you realize that it is beyond those acres or in your distant past, back in the realm of TiVo and cubicles, of take-out food and central heat and air, in that country where discomfort has nearly disappeared, that you were deprived. Deprived of the pleasure of desire, of effort and difficulty and meaningful accomplishment. A farm asks, and if you don't give enough, the primordial forces of death and wildness will overrun you. So naturally you give, and then you give some more, and then you give to the point of breaking, and then and only then it gives back, so bountifully it overfills not only your root cellar but also that parched and weedy little patch we call the soul.

This book is the story of the two love affairs that interrupted the trajectory of my life: one with farming—that dirty, concupiscent art—and the other with a complicated and exasperating farmer I found in State College, Pennsylvania.

Part One
Leaving

The first time I laid eyes on Mark, we were in the run-down trailer that served as his farm office and his home. I had driven six hours from Manhattan to interview him for a story I was pitching, about the young farmers who were growing the kind of local organic food that more and more people wanted to eat. I knocked on his front door during what turned out to be the after-lunch nap. When nobody answered, I let myself into the kitchen and called out, and after a minute the bedroom door banged open and Mark strode down the hallway, buckling his belt. He was very tall, and his long legs propelled him toward me with a sort of purposeful grace. He wore scuffed leather work boots, blue jeans gone white at the thighs, and a devastated white dress shirt. He had lively green eyes, a strong and perfect nose, a two-day beard, and a mane of gold curls. His hands were large and callused, his forearms corded with muscle and wide blue veins. He smiled, and he had beautiful teeth. I smelled warm skin, diesel, earth.

He introduced himself, shook my hand, and then he was abruptly gone, off on some urgent farm business, the screen door banging shut behind him, promising over his shoulder to give me an interview when he got back that evening. Meantime, I could hoe the broccoli with his assistant, Keena. I recorded two impressions in my notebook later on: First, this is a *man*. All the men I knew were cerebral. This one lived in his body. Second, I can't believe I drove all this way to hoe broccoli for this dude.

That first night, instead of doing an interview with him, I helped Mark slaughter a pig. I'd been a vegetarian for thirteen years, and I was wearing a new white agnès b. blouse, but he was shorthanded, and being on his farm without helping felt as unnatural as jumping into a lake and not swimming. I'd never seen an animal slaughtered before, and I could not look when he shot the pig—a sow named Butch with black-and-white spots, like a porcine character in a children's story. Once she was still I regained my equilibrium. I helped hoist the carcass on a gambrel and make the eviscerating cut from breastbone to belly, holding the steaming cavity open while Mark cut the organs free from their moorings. I was not disgusted but enlivened by what we were doing. I was fascinated by the hard white purse of the stomach, the neat coil of intestines, the lacy white caul fat, the still-bright heart.

After the carcass was halved we hauled it in a cart to a walk-in cooler near the road. One hundred yards from us was a development of grandly scaled houses on small lots. They had carefully clipped lawns, and geraniums in pots at the ends of the driveways. In the falling dark Mark draped the now-headless pink half body over his shoulder. It was bulky and heavy and awkward to carry, just like dead bodies on TV. I held on to the slippery back trotters and helped get the pig into the cooler and hung on a hook from the ceiling. The cars zipping by had their headlights on by then, and the lights were coming on in the houses across the road. I wondered if anyone could see us, and if they would call the police.

I stayed at a chain hotel in town that night and soaked the pig grease off of me in a bathroom that seemed shockingly white and sterile. I felt like I'd been on a long trip to a very foreign country.

The next morning I got up at dawn and went back to the farm. Mark's crew was gathered for breakfast: cornmeal pancakes and homemade sausage drizzled with warm maple syrup. I ate a double helping of sausage, and that was the end of my life as a vegetarian.

Mark disappeared again right after breakfast, the pig in the back of a borrowed Explorer, off to his Amish friends' butcher shop. He'd be back in the afternoon, he said, and we could conduct a proper interview then. In the meantime, I could rake rocks in the tomatoes with his other assistant, Michael.

Michael did not look optimistic about my work capacity. I had traded my white blouse for a vintage Cheap Trick T-shirt, tight jeans, and a pair of thrift-store Dingos with chunky little heels. It was the kind of ironic-chic outfit that worked well in the East Village but looked strange and slightly slutty in a field in Pennsylvania. I thought of myself as extremely fit and, as I phrased it to myself, *strong for my size*, which was a slight five two including the heels on the Dingos, even though my most vigorous exercise at that time came from regular games of pin-ball. I was already sore from the previous day's exertions, but I am cursed with a physical competitiveness that goes beyond reason. I inherited this trait from my father, who, by way of example, detached a hamstring attempting to muscle his way through a standing dock start while waterskiing at the age of seventy-three.

Michael handed me a hard-toothed rake, and we set off in adjacent rows. Penn State was just down the road, and Michael, a film major, had graduated that spring. He'd begun volunteering weekends at Mark's farm to see if, as he put it, hard work would make him a man. When he graduated, Mark had hired him full-time. Michael's father was an accountant and his girlfriend was about to start law school and the lot of them had a fairly dim view of farming and were hoping that Michael would soon get it out of his system.

I asked a lot of questions, to cover my puffing, and took every opportunity to lean on the rake in a pose of intense lis-tening. The July sun stung like a slap on the face and raised up around us the sharp, resinous smell of tomato. The plants were as tall as I was and heavy with fruit, held upright by twine and oak stakes. To a person used to growing nothing bigger than herbs in a window box, they seemed vaguely menacing. The soil between the rows was dry and clumped and heav-ily studded with rocks. Michael told me to ignore the rocks smaller than an egg and rake the rest into piles, then shovel the piles into a wheelbarrow to be dumped in the hedgerow. I was shocked by the weight of each shovel full of rocks, and I flipped the wheelbarrow on my first trip. Rake, shovel, dump.

Two interminable hours passed in this way, until it occurred to me that, if this went on much longer, I'd seize up entirely and be unable to depress the clutch in order to drive myself home. In desperation, I offered to go in to cook lunch for everyone. I tried to make the offer sound casual. I couldn't quite believe how much damage I'd done to myself in so short a time. There were blisters rising between my left thumb and first finger, I couldn't fully straighten my back, and my crotch, imprisoned in the tight jeans, felt chafed beyond repair.

I wasn't much of a cook back then. I appreciated good food, but I didn't have a steady relationship with it. Food was more like a series of one-night stands, set in front of me at a restaurant or delivered in little white cardboard containers by a guy on a bicycle. I wasn't sure the oven in my apartment was functional, since in the seven years I'd lived there, I'd never used it. The refrigerator worked, but in my small studio it was more valuable to me as storage space than as a kitchen appliance. I kept the dog's kibble in there, and a Brita pitcher of water, and, bookshelf space being dear, the Manhattan phone book, which in my memory of those years will always be heavy and cold. The freezer held a tray of shrunken ice cubes and a bottle of Polish vodka.

Mark's kitchen took up half the trailer and reminded me of a market in a third-world country. It was stuffed full of colorful and unpackaged things, the smells of milk and meat and dirt and vegetation mingling together in an earthy perfume that was strong but not unpleasant. I opened doors, peered cautiously at the high shelves. The cabinets held gallon jars of black beans and dried apples, wheat and rye berries, small, dry ears of corn.

The cupboard above the stove was full of bundles of herbs and unlabeled bottles of some fizzy, amber liquid. I opened the refrigerator and found an uncovered pot brimming with soft, bloody things I recognized as Butch's internal organs, and a wire basket of scuffed brown eggs. In the crisper were Ball jars of butter and cottage cheese, a pile of golf ball–looking things that may have been turnips, and some carrots, unwashed.

I quickly shut the refrigerator door and grabbed a basket and a knife and went back out to the field where Michael had finished raking rocks and was now busy mulching the rows of tomatoes with bales of half-rotted straw. I looked at all the food that was there for the picking. New potatoes, broccoli, lettuce, herbs, peas, beets, and blackberries. There was a cow grazing with her calf, a flock of hens pecking away at some compost, another pig rooting through a pile of leaf litter. Everywhere I looked, there was plenty. I felt some ideas moving around in my head, big and slow, like tectonic plates. This was only a six-acre plot, the size of a large playground, but there were vegetables here for two hundred families. It all seemed so much simpler than I'd imagined. Dirt plus water plus sun plus sweat equaled food. No factories required, not a lot of machinery, no poisons or chemical fertilizers. How was it possible that this abundance had always existed, and I had not known it? I felt, of all damn things, safe. Anything could happen in the world. Planes could crash into buildings, jobs could disappear, people could be thrown out of their apartments, oil could run dry, but here, at least, we would eat. I filled my basket with tomatoes and kale and onions and basil, calculating in my head the hefty sum all those vegetables would have cost at the farmers' market in New York City, and went back inside hoping to do them justice.

I found two tools in the kitchen that are so familiar to me now they're like old friends: a ten-inch soft steel chef's knife with a very sharp blade and a cast-iron skillet so big I could barely get my two arms around it. I set to work, cutting ribs out of the kale and chopping tomatoes and onions without knowing exactly where the meal was going. I did know that, if the rest of the crew was as hungry as I was, I had better aim for quantity. I heated the skillet on two burners and sautéed onion in butter, adding some diced carrots and the tomatoes and a bit of water to steam the kale. I covered the skillet with something that looked like a manhole cover, and when the kale was soft I dug shallow divots in it and cracked a dozen eggs into the holes to poach. Then I minced some garlic and basil together and mashed it into a knob of butter and spread that on slices of bread I'd found in the cupboard. I put the garlicky bread under the broiler, and just as the crew walked in from the field I pulled the tray of fragrant toasts out of the oven with a flourish, dealt pieces onto plates, topped them with the kale and poached eggs, and crowned each with a spoonful of cottage cheese and a grind of black pepper.

When we were all seated and served I took my first trepidatious bite, and then sat back. It was, I thought, astoundingly delicious—the kale a fresh, green backdrop to the hot, sharp bite of garlic and basil—and I felt very clever to have made it. I looked around the table, expecting raves and compliments, but there was only the flash of silverware, the purposeful movement of several jaws. "Please pass the salt," Michael said, eventually. It wasn't that my lunch was bad, I realize now. In fact I bet they thought it was pretty good. But pretty good is just not that impressive to farmers who eat like princes every day. Food, a French man told me once, is the first wealth. Grow it right, and you feel insanely rich, no matter what you own.

It was evening again before I managed to intercept Mark's orbit. Michael and Keena and a handful of volunteers who had been buzzing around the fields had all left for the day, but Mark was still working. I'd begun to wonder if this guy was ever still. Now he was literally running between jobs on those long legs of his, drawing on what seemed to be a boundless reserve of energy. He checked the irrigation in the carrots, jotted notes for the next day, bent to pull a clump of innocuous-looking weeds from the edge of the strawberries, tested the deer fence for charge and then baited it with cotton balls soaked in apple scent, so the deer would get a good, strong shock on the nose. I trotted along after him, juggling a notebook and pen with a screwdriver and pieces of broken hose that he absentmindedly handed me. He talked the whole time, at a pace and with a dexterity that surprised me. I thought farmers were supposed to be salt-of-the-earth-type people, not dumb, exactly, but maybe a little dull.

He didn't like the word *work*. That's a pejorative. He preferred to call it *farming,* as in *I farmed for fourteen hours today.* He did not own a television or a radio and figured he was probably one of the last people in the country to know about September 11. Still doesn't listen to the news. It's depressing, and there's nothing you can do about most of it anyway. You have to think locally, act locally, and his definition of local didn't extend much beyond the fifteen acres of land he was farming. The right thing was to try to understand how you were affecting the world around you. At first he'd been against just plastic, but he was becoming suspicious of any metal that he couldn't mine and smelt himself. In fact, when it was time to build himself a house, he'd like to build it with no nails, no metal at all, so that it could compost itself down to nothing after he was dead. He had never owned a car. He biked or hitchhiked where he needed to go. He had recently turned against the word *should,* and doing so had made him a happier person. He found the market economy and its anonymous exchange boring. He'd like to imagine a farm where no money traded hands, only goodwill and favors. He had a theory that you had to start out by giving stuff away—preferably big stuff, worth, he figured, about a thousand dollars. At first, he said, people are discomfited by such a big gift. They try to make it up to you, by giving you something big in return. And then you give them something else, and they give you something else, and pretty soon nobody is keeping score. There is simply a flow of things from the place of excess to the place of need. It's personal, and it's satisfying, and everyone feels good about it. This guy is completely nuts, I thought. *But what if he's right?*

Finally, I dropped the hose and the screwdriver and asked him to please stop moving and sit down with me so I could focus. I had to leave the next morning, and all I had so far were a few confused scribbles of notes and a sore crotch. He stopped moving and looked at me then, and laughed.

In the last hour of light we walked through the upper fields, past a pond and into a dense woods where chipmunks scuttled through their end-of-day rounds. We sat together on the trunk of a downed oak and the sudden stillness was like getting off a ship after a long voyage. When Mark tells the story of our relationship, this is the moment he counts as the beginning. Sitting on the log and answering my questions, he says, he began hearing a voice in his head, a persistent and annoying little voice, like a mental mosquito. "You're going to marry this woman," the voice was saying.

He did his best to ignore it. He wasn't looking for a girl-friend. He'd recently ended a long-term relationship. More-over it was high summer. He had a farm to run. He had to focus. The last thing he needed was this voice saying he'd been found by a wife. "You're going to marry this woman," the voice insisted, "and if you were brave enough, you'd ask her right now."

While Mark was considering whether or not to propose, I was considering narrative possibilities. Mark would be an interest-ing subject. He was well-read and articulate and he seemed to be something of a ham, the kind of natural performer who'd enjoy an attentive audience. He certainly generated a lot of dialogue. He had an original mind. I liked looking at his strong face and long limbs. It occurred to me that, instead of pitch-ing a magazine story about him, maybe I should pitch a book.

I'd have to spend a lot of time at the farm, of course, but I could sublet my apartment, find somewhere cheap to rent in the area. Maybe I could pitch a tent in the carrots.

When it was dark he walked me back to my car. He was talking again about the home he wanted to create. It would make him happy, he said, to haul his own water in wooden buckets, to wear clothes made of buckskin that he tanned himself. "And what does your female counterpart look like?" I asked. I was having a hard time imagining the woman who'd fit into Mark's future. To me, the buckets sounded heavy and the buckskin repellent. Mark told me later that he'd thought the question was wildly flirtatious. Neither of us remembers how he answered.

Before I pulled away Mark filled my backseat with vegetables, eggs, milk, pork, and butter, as though provisioning me for an expedition to some bleak wasteland. On the drive home I thought about him and also about the time I'd spent in the fields, hoeing broccoli, raking rocks. It had been hellish, and I wanted more of it. What was wrong with me? I chalked it up to creative energy. I'd mistaken fascination for love a few times in the past, but this was the first time I'd got it wrong the other way around.

It was past midnight by the time I got back to the city. I double-parked in front of my building and unloaded the crates of food Mark had sent back with me. It was a beautiful summer night, and the bars and restaurants and streets of my neighborhood were busy with young people dressed for a night out. Sitting there on the sidewalk, Mark's homey wooden crates full of food looked like something out of a different time. A man I recognized from the dog park walked by. Characteristically, we knew the names of each other's dogs but not of each other. "Wow," Bear's Owner said. "Been shopping?" he asked. "Nope," I said. "Been in the country." I thrust a dozen eggs at him, thinking of Mark and his idea of generosity. Bear sniffed at my crate of vegetables, and the guy looked confused. "They're organic," I said, by way of explanation. He walked away, holding the eggs gingerly. I rolled my eyes and got back in my car to circle the block, looking for a parking spot.

I lived on East Third Street, across from the Hells Angels headquarters. My apartment was a tiny studio with good light, and on Sunday mornings I liked to sit out on the fire escape and drink coffee and look down on a walled cemetery with nineteenth-century stones and spreading locust trees. I'd lived there since soon after I arrived in the city, before the East Village was fully gentrified, when there were still lots of junkies around and rent was five hundred dollars a month. The Angels always had a thug or two standing cross-armed, guarding the bikes that gleamed there in a long row. When I walked home past their door late at night, a certain muscle-bound Angel with a Zapata mustache would look me up and down and growl, "Get home safe," which I found comforting and kind of sexy until I saw the same guy knock a skinny messenger to the street with a baseball bat for bumping into his bike, then lift the bat above his head and bring it down hard. I ran around the corner before calling 911, because I was scared he would see me.

My building was an even mix of rent-controlled tenants who'd lived there forever and the youngish artists and hipsters who are the harbingers of gentrification. A middle-aged woman named Janet was ensconced on the second floor. She wore elaborate wigs and dresses left over from her glory days as a nightclub singer, and she lived at the window, our Argus, her pack of white toy poodles yipping in the background. Nothing came or went from our building without her comment. I found her vigilance comforting, too, but when the elevator was broken you'd walk past her door and the smell of poodle would waft out along with the sound of her shrieking at the dogs to shut up and you'd think of the word *squalor*.

I was dating in a way that can best be described as haphazard, shuffling drinks and dinners and movie dates with a filmmaker, an art collector, a political writer, and an ex. I assumed all of them had their own shuffles going on, too. We were all very busy and we were all very cagey about our feelings. If there was a chance for love, nobody was talking about it. Least of all me. I'd withstood a few heartbreaks by then, and I'd gotten the idea that emotional needs were unattractive in a woman, especially after the age of thirty. Safer, I thought, to play it tough and elusive.

Meanwhile I was trying to stave off an ache I'd developed. I noticed it first at the airport, coming home from a trip. There was a crowd on the other side of customs, holding flowers, the little kids dressed up and excited, waiting for their loved ones, who were returning home. I hated walking that gauntlet of waiting people, because none of them was waiting for me. I stood in the cab line and felt the weight of my aloneness come down on me. I unlocked the door of my apartment, where the only movement, while I was gone, had been the light moving across the walls from morning to evening and a scuttling roach or two, and the air inside smelled like loneliness. The ache eased a little the next day, after I'd picked up my dog from my sister, gotten sucked back into the slipstream of the city. But only a little. And soon it spread, until the word *home* could make me cry. I wanted one. With a man. A house. The smell of cut grass, sheets on the line, a child running through a sprinkler. This humble wish seemed to me so impossible. It was so different from the life I was living, and no one in my circle had those things, or wanted them, or would admit it if they did. I thought I could acknowledge the ache and learn to live with it, the way you learn to live with the pain that lingers long after you've broken a bone, the kind that foretells a shift in the weather.

I was busy the rest of the summer, writing ad copy, teaching a class, cobbling together freelance jobs, just scraping by. I was caffeinated and frazzled and worried about money, and, like most everyone else in New York, I accepted that as normal. The exception was the time I spent thinking about Mark and his farm. That place made me calm. I wanted to learn everything I could about what he did. I bought Wendell Berry's *The Gift of Good Land* and read it on the subway, scribbling notes in the margin. *What does a harrow look like? What is a Southdown?* By September I had decided I wanted to sublet my apartment, and spend a year in Mark's fields, and write about it. Then he called and left a message on my machine.

In the hours I'd spent writing and thinking about him, he'd

become more a character than a person to me. His real voice took me aback, because it sounded higher than the voice I'd been hearing in my head as I wrote. I had to play the message twice to register the gist of it, which was that he was inviting me to join him for a weekend at a real old-school, hoity-toity resort in the Catskills. The whole thing seemed criminally out of step for the ascetic and gritty farmer character I'd written, and my first thought was that I'd have to make some revisions.

Then I thought about whether I should accept. He'd said he had a free weekend for two coming to him, everything included, because the year before he'd taught a winter survival class at the resort. They were hosting a symposium of chefs and farmers, which he thought might be useful for my research. It *did* sound like a good opportunity for research. I wasn't deaf to the subtext. I was old enough to know that, when a man invites you to spend the weekend with him at a hotel, he's pretty much obliged to make a pass. Not doing so would be like bringing a gun out onstage and never shooting it. But Mark was so weirdly different from every man I'd ever met that I thought he might be an exception. And if not, I was from New York. I could handle myself with a *farmer,* for God's sake. I didn't want to blow all my plans with a fling, and clearly the last thing I needed was a long-distance relationship with some wing nut who didn't believe in nails. For insurance, I packed frumpy, old underwear and did not shave my legs.

I hit traffic on my way out of the city and arrived four hours late, nerves a-jangle, and found Mark tipped back in a chair near the reception desk, snoozing, with a giant straw hat over his face, the same one he wore in the field. The hat was stuck with turkey feathers and was truly enormous. This was more in keeping with the character I'd written, and I felt relief, followed quickly by mortification. In retrospect, I believe the hat may be exactly why I decided to order a second martini at our first dinner together, which led to the historically accurate fact that, despite my best intentions, I was the one who made the pass at him.

That night was the beginning of a profound and delightful education about lifestyle choices. Mark, I discovered, had never smoked or gotten drunk, he'd never tried drugs or slept around. He'd eaten wholesome and mostly organic food, and he'd spent most days of his adult life doing some kind of arduous physical exercise. He was the healthiest creature I'd ever laid eyes on. Some people wish for world peace or an end to homelessness. I wish every woman could have as a lover at some point in her life a man who never smoked or drank too much or became jaded from kissing too many girls or looking at porn, someone with the gracious muscles that come from honest work and not from the gym, someone unashamed of the animal side of human nature.

After that I stopped pretending I was doing research and recognized that some big life shift was under way. I scrapped the book idea and spent long weekends at Mark's farm. No heels, no notebook. Two new worlds were opening up to me. One was the work. I collected eggs and fed the chickens, exhausted myself with field work. I'd been all over the world as a travel writer, done all the things that people spend their money and their vacation days to do, and I couldn't think of anywhere I'd rather be or anything I'd rather be doing than pulling warm eggs out of a nest box.

The other new world was the food. Mark could cook. Hell, anybody could cook with the ingredients he had on hand—vegetables with the earth still clinging to them, herbs growing at arm's reach, a quality of eggs and milk and meat that you can't buy in any store. But Mark could *really* cook. When he was eleven his mother got sick of hearing the family complain about whatever she'd made for dinner, so she went on strike, and Mark and his little sister began cooking for the family. In the beginning there were failures, nights of clumpy macaroni with ketchup or wretched conglomerations of leftovers. But at that age Mark was weedy, hyperactive, and growing in spurts that could be measured in inches per month. He was constantly ravenous. Hunger is a great teacher, and Mark applied himself. He read *Mastering the Art of French Cooking,* and the more he succeeded the more ambitious he got. He became obsessed with rolling perfect sushi, and when he had a crush on a girl in middle school he cooked her a seven-course dinner. Eventually he ditched cookbooks and went freelance, adhering to a few simple principles: keep your knives sharp, taste everything, and don't be stingy with the salt. His love of food was part of what eventually led him to farming. The only way he'd be able to afford the quality of food he craved, he said, was to become a banker or grow it himself, and he couldn't sit still long enough to be a banker.

So there I was, eating haute cuisine in a mobile home. He cooked for me as seduction, as courtship, so that I'd never again be impressed with a man who simply took me out to dinner. And I fell in love with him over a deer's liver.

It was later that fall, before the first frost but far enough along in the season that a clear night would come with a strong chill on it. There was a moon rising, but it was only a sliver, and I was so fresh from the city that the stars standing out on a deep black sky were a novelty. Mark locked his dogs inside the trailer and pulled his rifle down from a high shelf. I had never held a rifle before, and the heft of it surprised me. I ran my hand over the smooth, dark wood of the stock and shivered.

Going for a walk at night is profoundly different from going for a walk at night with a gun. We crept along the path next to the strawberries, where the deer had been grazing, bringing our feet down softly, barely breathing. The air around us felt charged with danger and expectation. The deer population was high that year, and they'd been getting into his fields, despite the elaborate electric fences and the two dogs. He had nuisance permits that allowed him to hunt out of season, and also at night. Mark didn't hunt for the fun of it. He hunted to protect the plants, and for meat.

I carried the light. Mark kept the gun. I don't know how long we'd been out there, moving under a tense kind of trance, before he wordlessly passed the gun to me. I took it from him and pressed my eye to the sight, which was like a telescope with crosshairs. I swung it around to the hedgerow, and in the faint moonlight I saw a group of three deer, two young bucks with twiggy horns and a young doe, and was hit with a saturated mix of emotions. It was the awe you feel in the presence of a big, beautiful animal, a free and wild thing, plus a good dose of adrenaline, and also an eager feeling that I realized, with a kind of a jolt, must be some form of bloodlust. Instantly, my hands began to tremble so hard I could hear my bracelet rattle against the gun's stock. I lowered the gun and handed it to Mark, who raised it and took the shot. Through the dark I could barely make out the shapes of two animals galloping off into the woods.

The deer's liver was heavier than it looked like it should be, and firm, and as I held it under cold running water it still had the warmth of life in it. I watched Mark slice it thin, dust the slices with a little flour and salt and pepper, and lay them in a pan of sizzling butter, where a handful of minced shallots had already gone glassy and translucent. He ran out to the field and came back with a handful of mixed herbs, chopped them into a rough chiffonade, and tossed them into the pan. The liver slices still had a hint of pink to them when he pulled them out and laid them on a plate. To the pan he added a generous splash of the white wine I'd brought, and a cup or so of cream that he skimmed from the top of a gallon of milk. After it had bubbled there for a while and thickened, he put the liver slices back in and turned them once. Then he arranged them carefully on a pair of warm plates and spooned the cream sauce over them. He'd set the table with two candles, and a canning jar of wildflowers. There was a loaf of homemade bread, a salad of cold-hardy greens, and a wooden bowl of bright apples.

My mother is one of those people who seriously hates liver. I'd gotten the idea from her that it was something to be avoided at all costs, so I'd made it to that moment without ever tasting liver. That was probably a considerable blessing, because I was spared from eating the not-so-fresh supermarket variety, cooked to a tacky paste, that gives liver a bad name. And it added to the surprise and pleasure of that first profound bite. The texture reminded me of wild mushrooms, firm but tender, and the flavor was distinct but not overpowering, the wildness balanced between the civilized and familiar pairing of cream and wine. And there was something else about it, something more primal, a kind of craving, my body yelling, EAT THAT, I NEED IT. That was my first hint that there's a wisdom to the appetite, that if you clear out the white noise of processed food and listen, healthy and delicious are actually allies. We are animals, after all, hardwired to like what's good for us, and it makes sense that a vestigial part of us should still be crouched by a fire somewhere, smacking its lips over some nutritionally dense innards. That might have been the same deep part of me that first told me to love Mark. Don't be an idiot, it said. The man hunts, he grows, he's strapping and healthy and tall. He'll feed you, and his genes might improve the shrimpiness of your line. LOVE HIM.

That voice was a lot clearer in Pennsylvania than it was in Manhattan when Mark came to visit me for the first time. He took a bus, and I picked him up at Port Authority. He was wearing a stained red turtleneck, a tattered brown Carhartt jacket, and the omnipresent giant straw hat. It's hard to shock a New Yorker, but that hat parted the midtown crowd like a shark's fin, causing pedestrian pileups as people stopped to stare. I noted, with a certain satisfaction, that Mark looked at least as out of place in my city as I'd looked on his farm.

I'd been looking forward to his visit, but as soon as he arrived, I realized I had no idea what to do with him in the city. He hated bars, and he didn't see the pleasure of cafés, which ruled out both my nocturnal and my diurnal habitats. I tried to introduce him to the concept of hanging out with coffee and the *Times* on Sunday morning, but he didn't get it, and my apartment felt oppressively small with him moving spastically about in it. He wasn't impressed by the restaurants I took him to, because he considered the prices offensive when the food in his trailer was generally better. His legs were too long to fit comfortably in a theater seat. He was blind to the shabby coolness of my neighborhood and its denizens, the impressiveness of my friends' jobs and accomplishments. I couldn't take him to a party we were invited to in that turtleneck and hat. That left bookstores, which were mildly interesting to him, and pinball, which appealed to his competitive nature.

He liked taking taxis, because more often than not the driver would be from an agricultural village in some timeless quarter of the world, and Mark could engage him in a lively discussion of halal slaughter methods or the nuances of donkey harness or a particular village's strategies for controlling rat damage in stored grain. One Greek driver pulled over and turned off the meter to describe in detail the way they skinned sheep in his village, by cutting a slit in the skin of one leg and blowing it up like a balloon. A few weeks later Mark tried it, and it worked. What I learned from these experiences was that there were more cultural differences between Mark and me than there were between Mark and a random selection of taxi drivers from the developing world.

But there was always food. After his farm slowed down for the season, he came to New York every weekend. He'd arrive at my apartment with the now-familiar crates, stuffed full of heirloom winter squashes, fall greens, bundles of dry herbs, and roots. The phone book was relegated to the top of the bookshelf. Mark cleaned a mouse nest out of my oven and discovered that it worked. He unearthed plates and glasses I'd forgotten I owned and threw a cloth my sister had brought me from India over my desk to make a dining table out of it.

One night in November, I came home from teaching a class to find Mark had rearranged the furniture. My bed was in the center of the apartment, made up with fresh white sheets, and the desk-cum-table was next to the window, overlooking the cemetery, with a steaming pot of soup in the middle. It was cream of turnip, which sounds like the most unromantic dinner in the world, except that it was perfect, made with a Japanese variety called Hakurei, so sweet and mild they tasted like crisp white apples, and Mark's good homemade chicken stock, and farm-fresh cream. I'd contributed dessert: a bottle of very good port and a bar of the best dark chocolate I could find. It was an easy transition between the table and the bed, and I remember thinking that, if we could just box the city half of our relationship into this tight little triangle of stove, table, and bed, everything would be much easier. I have a picture from that night that I took of us in bed, with the camera held at arm's length, we two in the corner of it, the background the exposed brick of my apartment. When I look at it now it still takes my breath away, the beauty of his long, chiseled torso, the size of his callused hand over my breast.

That was the night he told me he wanted to leave the farm in Pennsylvania. He didn't own the land, and he couldn't build a house there, and so now that we'd met, there was no point in staying. He wanted me to leave the city, give up my lease, and go looking for land with him, for a place where we could build a home and a farm together.

We'd met in the summer, and started dating in the fall, and it wasn't quite winter yet. I thought I loved him, but I didn't even know him. He was asking me to leave behind all the friendships I'd cultivated, all the people I knew with similar backgrounds, educations, and interests. It broke my heart to think of leaving my sister, whose SoHo apartment was only a ten-minute walk from my own and whose proximity was the very best part of my city life. How could I not be close enough to turn up at a moment's notice for coffee or drinks, to Monday-morning-quarterback our latest relationship dramas? And there were my professional contacts, and my teaching gigs. Paltry though they were, they were what I had to hold on to. And he was asking me to burn the only bridge that could lead me back to Manhattan if things didn't work out between us: the lease on my affordable apartment.

He'd be giving up a lot, too. He'd built up a reputation in Pennsylvania, a customer base, a vital chain of connections. He'd invested in the infrastructure of his farm. But he was so forthright, and he seemed so extremely sure.

What he was holding out to me—home—felt so dear that

it set up some kind of vibration in me. He described it—fifty acres of good soil, a farmhouse with scrubbed wooden tables in a big kitchen, a pretty orchard, cows and horses in the pasture, and chickens running around the yard—until I could see it so clearly I could almost touch it. I told him, distractedly, that I'd lived with boyfriends before, and it seemed like a bad compromise, with all the tensions of a marriage and none of the benefits. But I don't want to be your boyfriend, he said, like it was the most obvious thing in the world. I want to be your *husband*.

I thought again that he was either crazy or right, and I figured the odds at about even.

After Mark went back to his farm, I met my friend James for a game of pinball at the Ace Bar on Fifth Street. It was four in the afternoon, and the bar was empty except for the skinny, tattooed girl bartender on whom James had a crush and a couple of dusty-looking alcoholics propped on opposing barstools. James and I were afternoon regulars there, and nobody minded that I brought my big shepherd mutt, Nico, who flew around the room, greeting everyone with a flapping tongue, dragging her leash through sticky pools of old beer. The pinball game was The Simpsons, my favorite, and I got multiball as I was telling James about the weekend, so that the news that I was leaving the city to be with the farmer was interrupted by dinging bells and the snaps of the flippers. James and I were in the same boat: freelancers who were no longer kids. We both came from the same kind of middle-class home, and had left behind its conventions, its rules and tastes and predictability. I think we both teetered between seeing the lives we'd made for ourselves as adventures and seeing them as disasters, and we took a certain comfort in each other's presence. When I told him I was leaving, he didn't believe me.

The same thing happened when I told my friend Brad. He was about to marry his girlfriend, and he was in the mood to believe in love, but this story of mine seemed a stretch. I couldn't blame him. It didn't even sound real to me until the fourth or fifth time I told it. My sister was just plain mad. "You're abandoning me," she said. I think my landlord was the only person who was overjoyed at the news that I'd be moving out at the end of the month. The East Village was booming, and he'd have the place renovated and the rent jacked up before the doorknob was cold.

Mark and I spent Thanksgiving with my family upstate. I'd edited my news a little, telling them of my intention to give up my lease, leave the city, and look for a farm with Mark, but leaving out any talk of marriage. My sister had met Mark in the city, and given him mixed reviews, which I'd assumed had been disseminated. I would be introducing him to my parents and my brother, Jeff, and his wife, Dani, who live in Virginia. Jeff is a naval officer, a pilot, not quite two years older than I. Earlier in his career his job was to stand on the deck of the aircraft carrier to direct landings, making life-or-death judgments about the incoming pilot's approach. In other words, he is a serious, logical, and entirely reliable person without many disconcerting quirks.

We arrived loaded with food. I was full of the zeal of the newly converted, eager to show off the gorgeous vegetables my boyfriend had grown—Brussels sprouts still on the stalk, sweet potatoes, beets, winter squash with flesh the color of ripe mangoes. Mark had helped his Amish friends slaughter turkeys that week, and he'd brought us one, plus a jar of his yellow, homemade butter. I'd forgotten how very clean my mother's world is until we walked in with those boxes, which were smudged with field dirt, a few limp leaves clinging to their bottoms. It appeared we would contaminate any surface we put them on, so Dad directed Mark to the garage, and my mother asked me quietly if I was sure it was safe to eat the turkey, which was wrapped in a drippy white shopping bag, its headless neck sticking out obscenely. I'd also forgotten that my mother *prefers* her food highly packaged, associations with its origins as obscured as possible. When we were kids, she would never buy brown eggs, because they seemed too "farmy."

Mark looked barely more trustworthy than the turkey. He'd come straight from the field, where his last act had been to harvest the food we were carrying. He could have used a haircut and a shave. He was wearing a threadbare T-shirt, inside out. (He believes shirts should be worn exactly as they appear out of the laundry—inside out or inside in. "They'll be right every other time. They wear more evenly that way.") "Well, he has a very nice smile," my mother said, when we were alone. Mark slept in the guest bedroom, and I slept in my girlhood bed, surrounded by my old books and a framed copy of my college diploma, which seemed to stare accusingly at me from the wall. "I didn't educate you for this," it said.

On Thanksgiving morning Mom ceded her kitchen to this stranger, this tall and wild-looking man, and he proceeded to cook with total abandon. He started at six, before the rest of the house was up, rummaging through drawers for utensils, making himself perfectly at home. By seven, as people began emerging from bedrooms in search of coffee, he was cooking his heart out, six dishes going at once, food flying around him like wood chips around a chain saw. In his enthusiasm, he'd trashed Mom's immaculate kitchen, splashing cream on the wall, treading bits of potato into the floor. I ran interference between the beets and the white carpet nearby, and at noon on the dot I opened the wine and poured Mom a big glass.

At three, the turkey came out of the oven, and it was glorious, skin crisp and perfectly brown, worthy of a cookbook centerfold. Mark had wrapped up his cooking early and had been out in the backyard with Dad and Jeff, splitting firewood. I'd watched his strong body out the window, bringing the ax down on the wood like a force of nature, never hurried, never resting. He split the wood from an entire tree, and then he came back in to make the gravy, stirring flour into the drippings in the pan, then stock and wine and herbs. Dani came to the stove to taste it, and her eyes got wide. "This gravy makes my nipples hard," she whispered to me. Then we all sat down, and the food worked that kind of magic on the whole family.

It was a simple meal, without flourishes, the kind of cooking that lets the food speak for itself. My mother declared it the best turkey she'd ever tasted, and said she was going to buy organic potatoes from now on. For Mark, food is an expression of love—love of life, and love for the people around him—all the way from seed to table. I think my family could taste how deep his love ran, and between the squash pie and another glass of wine, they decided—even as he talked freely about his desire to live in a money-free economy, in a house without nails—that it was possible, just possible, that I had not come completely unhinged. "Well, he's the best one she's brought home so far," I heard my brother mumble to my sister over coffee. It wasn't a perfect beginning, but they'd decided to give him a chance.

Mark drove back to the city with me to help me pack and move. I was in a profound state of giddiness, exactly the way I feel when I'm on a plane pointed somewhere far away and foreign, just before the wheels leave the tarmac. We sorted through my belongings and made a big pile of the ones Mark said I wouldn't need in my new life, and a tiny pile of things to bring along. I didn't want to leave behind my bed, which I'd spent a pile of money on, and loved. "Don't worry," Mark said. "I'll make you a new one, and it'll be so much more beautiful than this one, and it will be more special, because it will be hand-made." So we hauled mine downstairs to Janet's and helped her throw out her old one, which smelled of poodle, and tossed my keys inside my apartment and closed the door on all of it.

We moved an hour and a half up the Hudson, to New Paltz, where Mark had grown up and where his parents and sister still lived. We rented from his parents half a house, the house his grandmother lived in until she died. It was tucked into the elbow of a winding mountain road, and it had an old barn in the back stuffed with family artifacts: blueprints of the high-rise Manhattan buildings Mark's grandfather designed, boxes of papers, heavy furniture. The woods rose up behind the barn, and behind the woods was the Shawangunk Ridge and on it a knobby rock proboscis called Bonticou Crag. A few days after we moved in Mark took me for a hike up the cliffs behind the house. It was January, and the rocks were icy, and my dog, Nico, who was used to sidewalks, scrambled to keep up. We got to the top, and Mark, nearly mute with nerves, officially asked me to marry him. I watched a hawk circling in the clear, cold sky beneath us. The wind was vicious; the view was spectacular. I said yes. When I called my family to tell them the news, my parents weren't quite able to mask their alarm at what they were calling "a hasty decision," and my brother actually asked, "To whom?" My sister-in-law pointed out that a long engagement is a good thing because it allows a couple to really test each other out, and my sister, Kelly, said directly that, if this was what I wanted to do, I should go ahead, because divorce is always an option.

The house in New Paltz was supposed to be a layover, a place to base ourselves while looking for the embodiment of that vision Mark had presented to me—land, farmhouse, orchard. In my preflight giddiness, I'd imagined the layover would be brief. The bad news was that it was a terrible time to be looking. New Paltz was absorbing a surge of post–September 11 emigrants from the city, and the housing boom was in full swing. Land prices were soaring. The farms we saw were selling for

$25,000 per acre, and the soil was nothing to brag about. It started to look like it might be a hellishly long layover.

This was the first time that Mark had been without a farm since college, and without the constant hard physical work, he was wound up tighter than a border collie without a flock to herd. His obsessive side flourished unchecked. He wanted to live without electricity, but since he couldn't rip the wiring out of the house his parents owned, he decided we would simply not use it. He bought dozens of candles and got pissed off if I flipped on a light switch. He built a compost toilet out of a bucket full of peat moss, a toilet seat, and a wooden crate and installed it in the middle of the living room. When I protested he grudgingly added a screen. He learned to spin wool and spent hours at it until he could make fine, thin yarn. There was a neighbor with an outdoor wood-fired oven, and Mark took it over, turning out forty loaves of dense bread a week, which he would drop like bricks on the neighbors' doorsteps. He rode his bike to New Jersey and back.

When we'd been engaged for a month, we invited my parents to come for a visit, to meet Mark's parents. My father is a staunch Republican and an Air Force veteran, and in his retirement his politics have slipped further and further to the right. He doesn't believe in global warming, which to his mind is a tree-hugger scam or a UN plot, perpetuated, in either case, by the liberal media. My mother is a dozen years younger than he is, the same generation as Mark's folks, but when she married my father she graduated directly from Elvis and poodle skirts to martinis and easy listening, skipping the Beatles entirely. She would be mortified if you ever caught her without the beds made, the furniture dusted, and fresh vacuum cleaner marks on all the carpets. She has never been seen in public without makeup, her hair neatly styled.

If my parents are what Mark's parents would call *bourgeois,* then Mark's parents are what my parents would call *flakes.* They left New York City in the late 1960s for a shaley piece of ground in the Catskills and began learning to grow and raise their own food. They lived in a converted barn, and until Mark was born, they didn't have indoor plumbing. Mark's father was trained as an engineer, but he became a carpenter, a community activist, and later, a farmer. Mark's mother is a naturalist. Open her freezer and you'll usually find a dead woodchuck or some unlucky bird that brained itself against a window, awaiting a recreational dissection. At a party, I've seen her pull out her guitar and initiate—with no trace of irony—a round of "Kum Ba Ya."

At the dinner to celebrate our engagement, Mark's mom read a poem she'd written in our honor called "Bombs Are Falling in Iraq," which was met with steely silence from my parents across the table. The bad mood that came over the six of us was as heavy as the bread we were eating. Mark was deep into the No Lights phase, and after dinner my father groped his way out to the car for a flashlight to give to my mother so she could find her way to the bathroom, where she testily flipped on the lights.

Weeks dragged into months, and we were sleeping on a mattress on the floor. Mark didn't seem in any hurry to make me that beautiful bed, and every time I lay down I felt a little wave of bitterness.

I tried to buoy my sinking heart with the vision that had propelled me out of the city—the farmhouse, the orchard, the pastures full of happy animals—and I decided I might as well use this layover to gain some skills that would be useful to me in that new life. I read books about beekeeping and acquired a hive. Mark helped me create a chicken coop in the backyard, and I combed the livestock section of the classifieds until I found what I was looking for: eight Barred Rock hens, free to a good home.

The flock had come with a rooster, the mean kind. He had the giant spurs of an old-timer, and a crafty nature. He'd been thrown in as a bonus, but he was a major liability. He liked to attack from behind, and once, he trapped me in a corner of the greenhouse and hit me so hard with his spur my shin bled. I got so nervous I started carrying a broom with me every time I went outside. Mark thought this was hilarious. "He weighs five pounds," he said. "I think you can take him."

I searched the chicken chat rooms and learned that the only real cure for a mean rooster's meanness is to convert him to coq au vin. Mark held him upside down and I had the big sharp knife poised at his throat, but the thought of cutting him made me physically weak. When I finally did it, it was with a halfhearted stroke, which made for not such a good death, and I was haunted afterward by the flopping and squawking mess I'd made of the job. If I was ever to do it again, I decided, I wanted to have the skills to do it right. I made inquiries, and found two women in town who were about to slaughter their backyard flock. I asked if I could join them, in the spirit of research, and they agreed.

Jana and Suri were in their fifties, dressed in Birkenstocks and tie-dye, old friends from back in their commune days. They weren't farmers but had always raised some of their own food. Unlike Mark, who was utterly prosaic about such things, they believed that slaughter is a sacred act and wreathed the whole thing in improvised ceremony. When I arrived, they lit a bundle of sage and wafted its smoke around me. Then they hung a sheet between the chopping block and the coop, so the living chickens wouldn't be subjected to a preview of their demise.

Jana yanked a chicken out of the coop by its feet, and before she laid it down on a tree stump and chopped off its head with a hatchet, she cradled it in her arms like a baby. "Thank you, Chicken," she intoned. "Thank you for giving us your meat to feed our families. We are grateful. You nourish us. Now let your spirit fly up, up to Father Sun." Whack. Two or three birds went down this way, and then she handed me one. I held the chicken up by its legs, so that we were eye to eye. Its feathers opened, and it stopped flapping and kind of passed out. I cleared my throat. I couldn't bring myself to commend its spirit to Father Sun, but I could feel the weight of what I was about to do—take life from a healthy, sentient creature that would much prefer to stay alive, if it had a choice—and I felt grateful, sincerely grateful. "Um, Chicken?" I said. It blinked its strange eyes slowly in its rubbery mask of a face. "Sorry about this. I hope it's quick. Thanks a lot." Whack.

I did get better at chicken slaughter that day, and Jana and

Suri were very nice to me, and gave me the first bird I killed to take home for the oven. I cooked it and ate it with the reverence that comes from understanding the whole picture, an appreciation that can be expressed equally well, I decided, with ceremonial sage or with the careful preparation and enjoyment of an exceptional sage *stuffing*.

Meanwhile, we weren't getting any closer to finding a farm. What we needed, Mark said, was a big piece of good land that we could live on, that we could farm exactly as we wanted to, with the possibility of building a permanent home there. He wanted it to come for free. It would come, he explained, because he has had around him, since childhood, this thing he calls a magic circle, a kind of aura of luck that attracts the right thing at the right time. Good things had always come to him, and the farm would come, too. He didn't think it would take more than nine months, as long as I didn't dim his magic circle with my practical ideas, my negativity. It was an extremely exasperating situation.

The longer the search dragged on, the more we irritated each other. The first mad flush of love had cooled, and we were discovering how deeply different we were. Beneath my bohemian crust he found I was the fairly predictable product of my middle-class upbringing. I believed in the uplifting nature of manicures or a pair of new shoes. And under Mark's protean exterior, I was finding layer upon layer of unreconstructed hippie. I learned he'd spent his sophomore year in college, including the entire eastern Pennsylvanian winter, barefoot. I noticed that the unmasked pungency of his armpits made other people roll down the car window. I suspected that if we'd met at a different time in our lives we would have run as fast as possible away from each other.

Two things saved us. I got back-to-back travel writing gigs that kept us on different continents for several months. And then a generous and enthusiastic man named Lars Kulleseid wandered into Mark's magic circle. He was the father of a friend of Mark's sister, and by the end of our first meeting, he'd offered us a free lease on a big piece of good land he owned way up north on Lake Champlain. We were welcome to farm it any way we saw fit, and he was open to the possibility of having us build a permanent home and farm there. It was nine months to the day from the time our search began.

We saw Essex Farm for the first time on a blustery day in September. We'd taken the slow train north from Poughkeepsie with our bicycles and camping gear stashed in the luggage car. We bumped along the Hudson, into the Adirondack Park, past Lake George, to the deserted station at Westport, on the shore of Lake Champlain. The leaves in the Adirondack Mountains to the west had begun to turn, and the summer people from New York and Boston had already closed their houses along the lake and returned to the city. We biked along the wooded road north, hugging the shore of the lake, past an eclectic mix of blue-collar ranch houses, modest summer cottages, and opulent estates.

Lars was a lawyer in Manhattan and had bought the

five-hundred-acre farm as an investment eight years earlier, because, he said, he liked land, and because it touched the boy in him who had spent happy summers on his grandmother's farm in Norway. Since he'd owned it, it had been tended by a caretaker. He had not been visiting the farm as often as he thought he would. He had been considering selling it when we came along, but our roughly sketched idea of what we might do there had interested him enough to offer us a year's free lease of the farmhouse, barns, land, and equipment, if we found the land acceptable.

Following Lars's map, we biked through tiny Essex, past its blocks of 1850s houses that look pulled from a history book, the quaint ferry dock, the old stone library, and the brief row of Main Street shops, all closed up for the season. The farm began west of town, just past the firehouse. Our first glimpse, through the twilight, was of overgrown fields and a stretch of barbed-wire fence badly in need of repair. Some people were furiously cutting hay out there, two tractors racing the dark.

We found the dirt driveway between two curving stone pediments, the eastern one supporting a faded green sign that read "Essex Farm." The driveway was bordered with maple saplings, their leaves turned red, and the grass was neatly trimmed, but the farmhouse, a quarter mile in, had peeling white paint and a sagging roof. The front window was cracked, which made the house look like it was blind in one eye. We paused in front of the house to get our bearings, and suddenly a muscular black pit bull shot out of the garage, followed by a pair of white shepherd mutts. The pit bull hit the end of his chain and flipped backward, revealing a giant pair of testicles.

The white dogs seemed less homicidal and cringed and circled around our legs. We could hear a television blaring football from the open upstairs window, but nobody answered our knock. We continued along the long drive, lined on both sides with buildings on the verge of collapse. Just off the driveway, a school bus stuffed with old plastic bread crates was sinking into the dirt.

We wheeled our bikes into the granary. The floor was two inches deep in old grain, and when we opened the door the light cut through the dust and sent a battalion of rats scuttling for their exits. We left the bikes and walked east, back toward the lake. We were on a slight rise and could see that the farm was a mosaic of open fields and stands of nursery trees— spruce, pin oak, linden, and red maple—planted in straight rows. The land was flat, and some of it tended toward swamp. We pitched our tent among a bunch of arborvitae. The white dogs had followed us, begging for attention.

By the time the tent was pegged down it was nearly dark. We retrieved our bikes and retraced the last part of our ride, back into the village of Essex. I was bone tired, and still jet-lagged from a recent trip to Asia, and the only thing I wanted more than sleep was food. For some reason we'd failed to bring provisions, and my blood sugar was dropping below the level required to keep me sane. I wanted food like a wolf wants food. I wanted food so bad I was angry about it. I sat on a bench outside the town hall while Mark went to explore our options. When he returned he sat down and put his arm warily around me before delivering the bad news: the only place to eat was the Inn, and they wouldn't take us, despite the empty tables I could see through the window, because we didn't have a reservation. There were no stores, and the next town was a five-mile ride away, mostly uphill. It was fully dark by then, and I didn't think I could make it back to the farm, let alone the next town, without something to eat. I seethed, hating every quaint corner of a place so small and stupid you could actually starve to death in it. I hated the farm at that point, too. It was a dump, and it was swampy, and in the summer you'd probably be eaten alive by mosquitoes. I considered whether or not I'd be arrested if I were to sleep on the bench and decided I wanted to be arrested, because they'd be required to give me a ride to the jail in a car, and feed me. It'd probably be something perfectly acceptable, like peanut butter sandwiches. The only traffic light in town blinked endlessly to an empty street.

We were fixed in that tableau of misery by the glare of a pair of headlights pulling into the parking space in front of our bench. A man with silver hair got out, carrying a covered casserole dish. He smiled widely at us, noted our bicycles, asked us where we were from and where we were going. Mark told him we'd come up from Poughkeepsie and were camping at the Essex Farm. "Well," he asked, "are you hungry?" Even in my desperation, I could feel the "No, thanks," on the tip of my tongue, the city habit of distrust toward any show of unsolicited kindness. But Mark had already accepted on our behalf, and the man led us across the street to the basement of a big stone church and opened the door onto the sounds of clattering silverware and chatter and laughter rising up from a sea of gray hair.

It looked like we were crashing some kind of geriatric mixer, but I didn't care, because I had caught sight of the long tables against the wall, crammed with food. I could see plates of sliced ham, baked beans, mashed potatoes, and bright-colored Jell-O salads studded with fruit and topped with blobs of pastel Cool Whip. The man who'd brought us asked for everyone's attention, and fifty lined faces turned toward us. He introduced us as traveling long-distance bicyclists who wouldn't mind some dinner, and the room erupted in applause. The next thing I knew, someone had me by the elbow, guiding me through the crowd toward the tables laden with calories, placing a plate in my hands, pouring me a glass of iced tea. I wondered briefly if I was stuck in a dream, if this was some kind of cruel mirage, but soon I was seated and eating. It was the kind of food that grandmothers make, the kind invented to fill the stomach of a ditchdigger or a farmhand. I ate biscuits and gravy, green beans with slivered almonds, a drumstick of fried chicken. There was an urn of hot coffee, too, and an entire table dedicated to desserts.

When my peripheral vision returned and I could speak again, I learned that we'd stumbled into the centennial celebration of Essex's Methodist church. There weren't many young families in Essex, it turned out, and they were Episcopal. Everyone in that basement knew one another intimately, and most were in some way related. Many of the people I met that night would become important in our lives. The man who found us on the bench was Wayne Bailey. A few years later his wife, Donna, would knit a pink sweater with white piping for our infant girl, with a little cap to match. The small and wrinkled woman we sat next to was Pearl Kelly. She told us that night that she loved bicycling, and until she turned ninety and could no longer get her leg over the bar, she'd bike from her house to the ferry, for a joyride across the lake. Three years later I was milking a cow when her daughter-in-law came out to our barn to tell me Pearl had died. She had farmed all her life just down the road from us. Her vegetable stand is still there, paint chipping, its ridgepole succumbing to gravity.

We went back to the farm that night fed and warm in all ways, carrying pieces of cake wrapped up in napkins. I was entirely unused to that sort of common kindness. I didn't think that communities like this were supposed to exist anymore, in a country isolated by technology, mobility, and work. This was a place where neighbors took care of each other, where well-being was a group project, and I felt, again, that teary sense of safety I'd felt when I'd first looked out at Mark's fields full of food. It was a sappy and unironic feeling and a vestigial part of me protested against it, and then gave in.

We set off the next morning through a cold drizzle, with a shovel we'd found in the pole barn. For someone accustomed to living in a three-hundred-square-foot apartment, with a line of sight limited to the width of an avenue and whose largest ready unit of measure is the block, five hundred acres is unimaginably vast, not a farm but a fiefdom, a nation-state. On Lars's map, the property was a big square bordered by roads, each side a mile long, with chunks and bits cut out where land and lots had been sold off over the years.

As we walked, I fell into a dark mood, which I tried to blame on the weather and the fact that I hadn't yet had any coffee, but the truth was I'd gotten my hopes up, and the farm, under the filtered morning light, was disappointing. It didn't match the farm I'd imagined at all. It was supposed to be moderately hilly, with patchwork fields and well-kept buildings. It wasn't supposed to be nearly this big, or this remote. And it was definitely not supposed to be swampy.

We walked north first, our feet leaving wet impressions in the saturated soil. We climbed a rickety fence, crossed a scrubby wood, and found ourselves in the fifty-acre hayfield that had been cut the night before. I could feel coarse stubble pressing up through the bottoms of my boots. Mark stepped the shovel into the ground, and the soil under the sod was pure clay. I knew enough to recognize that this was not good. In a wet year it would drown roots, and in a dry year it would crack and harden into something resembling concrete. Soil that heavy would compact under the weight of machinery, squashing out the oxygen. Mark's mood drooped down to meet mine.

We backtracked to the two main barns, hulking red structures with cavernous mows. The main floor of the east barn had a low ceiling, and Mark had to duck to miss hitting his head on the beams. The west barn was airier and roomier, its heavy beams hand-hewn. Both barns were fitted out for dairy farming, the west one for milking, the east with tie stalls for calves and young heifers. There hadn't been animals there for decades, but the dairy records were still in a box in the milk house, a stack of cards with the names of long-dead cows penciled across the top in careful block letters. Kicking through piles of dusty hay in the west barn's mow, we found caches of empty beer bottles and faded, old packs of Kools. The roofs were tight on both main structures, but there was a large cement-block addition tacked on to the west barn, and its metal roof banged loosely in the wind, and the rain trickled through in several places, making a series of sad little waterfalls.

We crossed another rickety fence and found ourselves standing in an odd forest made up of hundreds of rows of stunted spruce trees growing in plastic pots. There had been a tree nursery on the farm after the dairy closed, and the trees had been growing like that for twenty years. They'd sent taproots through the holes in the bottoms of the pots and survived, but barely. There was a collapsed greenhouse back there, too, with the nursery firs and arborvitae growing up through scraps of pressure-treated wood and rotting plywood. That acreage had an apocalyptic feel to it, the slow force of the trees quietly softening all the square angles of human endeavor.

The farm's general flatness was relieved to the west by a steep rise covered in fifty acres of woods. We found a road cut through the trees, and Mark pointed out that the majority of the trees were healthy and sizable sugar maples. He looked along the trunks until he found old scars, where the trees had been tapped, and we realized we were walking through the farm's sugar bush. On our way back down we passed the sugarhouse, a three-sided barn with sagging walls. Someone had used it for a cow shelter, so it was full of old manure. The roof had leaked down into the evaporator, which had rusted into junk.

We saw the fields to the south last. These fields ran along

the busiest road, and half their acreage was taken up with over-grown nursery trees—fir, pin oak, and linden—that had been planted close and in rows. Mark stepped the shovel into the soil again and pried it up, and reached his hand into the cold cut he'd made. The shovel hadn't encountered any rocks, and the soil was the color of coffee, and its texture wasn't any-thing like the clay we'd uncovered earlier. He squeezed it in his hand, stroked his thumb over it, smelled it, and finally reached out his tongue and tasted it. It was a silty loam, a soil so rich and good it makes a farmer weep, and it ran for a quarter mile along the southern edge of the farm before turning once again to clay.

I think Mark fell in love with the land at that moment, with the same certainty and speed he had fallen in love with me. From then on, there was no question in his mind that this would be our home. Though it's hard for me to imagine now, he had to talk me into it. It wasn't the isolation or the clay that bothered me. "It feels like the farm has no soul," I said, when we were on the train ride home. "That's because it's not being used," Mark said. "It's just sleeping. You'll see." There was no time for dithering. It was late fall, and if we were going to grow anything the next spring, we'd need winter to plan and prepare. I thought about our other option—another year in New Paltz, looking—and decided to give it a go.

Part Two
Winter

We drove out of New Paltz headed due north. Squeezed into my tiny hatchback, among our boxes and bags, were my dog, Nico, the hens, and the humming hive of bees, its openings covered over with tape. The dog eyed the hive, the chickens eyed the dog, and if the bees weren't nervous then they were the only ones. When we entered the Adirondack Park all traffic fell away, and the mountains rose up around us, covered in pine and already tipped with frost. The light became thin and oblique, the billboards disappeared, the landscape grew wilder, the houses farther and farther apart until they disappeared from view. And then we arrived.

During the weeks we were away from it, and in the excitement of moving, the farm had gotten better in our imaginations. In theory, it was an adventure. Up close, it was frightening. Mark's friend Rob helped us move, driving up behind us in his big panel truck. Rob is a vegetable farmer, a hard worker, and an optimist. When he saw the state of the farm, and the size of the fields, he got very quiet.

The farmhouse was rented out until spring, so we moved our things into a furnished rental in town, a house with good nineteenth-century spirit but pitifully little insulation. Rob, with his farmer's sense of generosity, had brought us bags of winter squash, potatoes, carrots, leeks, and onions, and we stored them in the basement. That night there was an early snow falling, and Rob and Mark and I sautéed onions with cubed squash and potatoes for the kind of simple, comforting supper that helps make a new place feel like home. After the dishes were cleared, we lingered over a bottle of wine, talking about our plans. We were building a farm from scratch, and the land was big enough, and good enough, to support anything we could dream up. We had eighteen thousand dollars in savings between us, not much, but Lars's offer of a free year's lease included land, equipment, and a place to live. Like the size of the farm itself, the sheer breadth of possibility was both exhilarating and terrifying.

Mark had been musing a long time about the kind of farm he wanted to create. He'd been trained on vegetable farms, and vegetable growing was what he knew best. His farm in Pennsylvania ran on the CSA model, wherein members buy shares in the farm at the beginning of the season and get weekly distributions of the farm's produce. CSA stands for community supported agriculture, and the concept came from Japan via Europe in the 1980s. There is a lot for a farmer to love about CSA. It can be an effective way to cut out all the middlemen and market directly to your consumer. Moreover, since CSA members pay up front, income is predictable and there is good cash flow when farmers need it most, at the beginning of the growing season. CSA also lined up with Mark's impatience with the anonymity of the cash economy. He knew the people who were eating his food, they knew him, and they came to know the other members, so that distribution days became more like social events than like grocery shopping. Mark liked the model, but he had begun to feel that it wasn't enough. CSA farms focused almost entirely on vegetables and left out the foods that actually provide the majority of our calories, the grains and flours, dairy products, eggs, meats. In Pennsylvania, he'd tried to make some of those things available to his members by bringing in products from neighboring farms, but that system was a logistical nightmare, and the constant phone calls and travel time took him away from farming. Since he left Pennsylvania, he'd been wondering what it would be like to tweak the CSA model a bit, so that, instead of providing a set amount of vegetables each week, our farm would produce a whole diet, available to the members on an unlimited basis, just as it was available to us.

One of the gorgeous and highly annoying things about Mark's personality is that, once he bites into an idea, he'll worry it to death, exploring every possibility, expanding it to the point of absurdity and then shrinking it back down, molding it around different premises, and bending logic, when necessary, to cram it into a given situation. No matter what he is doing or saying or thinking, the idea is perking away in the background of his formidable brain, details accruing. Bits of it will surface, iceberglike, in a burst of chatter, but the bulk of it remains hidden until the whole thing appears at once, fully formed and fiercely defended.

By the time we'd gotten to Essex, his notion of a whole-diet CSA was complete. He wanted to build a farm that was so diversified it could supplant the supermarket, the kind of farm our great-grandparents' generation grew up on, but built big enough to feed a community instead of just a family. We would produce everything our members needed, beginning with the edible—a variety of meats, eggs, milk and dairy products, grains and flours, vegetables, fruits, and at least one kind of sweetener—but expanding, eventually, to include all the other things a farm could provide, like firewood and building materials, and exercise and recreation. The farm itself should be a self-sustaining organism, producing, as much as possible, its own energy, fertility, and resources. He wanted to make sure we organized the farm around the types of things we liked to do. For him, that meant as much physical work as possible, choosing hand milking over machine milking, for example, whether it made sense to the rest of the world or not. He still liked the idea of a cash-free economy, but he recognized the need for capital, in the start-up phase at least. Members would pay us one price up front, and there would be a sliding scale for low-income members that would slide all the way down to zero.

In order to create such a diversified farm by spring, we would need to work quickly, build up our infrastructure, figure out how to raise six different types of livestock and integrate them with the vegetable and grain rotations, the pastures and hayfields. We needed to figure out cash flow and labor. We would need to begin, he'd decided, with a milk cow. But first, we'd need to clean up. When Mark stopped talking, Rob just shook his head.

I didn't understand enough about farming at that point to grasp how audacious this plan was. And I still harbored a little of the urbanite's hubris, the feeling that with my education and worldly experience something as simple as *farming* couldn't possibly tax me all that much. In the abstract, the idea appealed to me in a way that was almost literary. It sounded romantic, and it resonated with that vision of home that I'd held on to on my way out of the city. It sounded like we'd be building an iconic family farm, only we'd be feeding a rather large extended family.

In truth, I probably would have agreed to anything, as long as it contained my favorite part of Mark's plan to make the farm energy-independent: draft horses. He'd never farmed with them before, but he'd gotten to drive teams a few times at other farms. He was no big fan of the tractor. He didn't like the smell of diesel, or the noise of engines; he didn't value the time he spent sitting on tractors, and he really didn't like fixing them. He liked the idea that animals could do everything tractors could do, and they could harvest their own fuel, too. He had seen enough prosperous Amish farms in Pennsylvania to know that draft animal power is far from a kooky idea, that given the right context, and the right scale, horses make good sense.

Thinking about having horses in my life again was like thinking about a place you'd been when you were young and untroubled, a place so happy that remembering it was almost painful. I was born with an affinity for horses, and all my early memories are suffused with them. I begged my way into riding lessons when I was seven, and when I was fourteen my parents bought me a sturdy little Morgan mare. I kept her at a neighbor's barn a mile from our house, and she was the counterweight to everything that's awkward and horrible about adolescence. I'd never driven a team before, never used a horse for any sort of work, but I was confident around horses. I knew what made them tick. I'd left behind everything that was familiar to me—my friends, the city, the rules of urban engagement—for this unknown new life, this compelling man whose sanity I sometimes questioned. The promise of horses, at least, was an anchor to hold on to.

The outbuildings had filled, over generations, with the kinds of bits and pieces that a line of frugal farmers judged prudent to save: picked-over engines, scabbed chunks of metal, quarter sheets of plywood gone crumbly with rot. In one corner of the machine shop, there was a paint bucket of bent tenpenny nails, waiting for the day when someone would have the time to bang them straight. There were piles of parts from several generations of milking machines—rubber teat claws, buckets, pieces of vacuum systems—and a shed stuffed full of sunbleached four-gallon plastic pots, too brittle to use, from the farm's days as a tree nursery. On a nail in the leaning pole barn, there was a horse's collar, its straw stuffing poking out, a vestige of the last time there'd been animals at work on the farm. Pieces of metal had collected around the buildings like sand on a reef: the tailgate of a pickup, a cartoonlike section of chain with eight-inch links, several road signs, patches cut out of them with a torch. We spent long days sorting through these things, filling the derelict school bus with metal for the scrap man, filling a Dumpster with the trash. We made a stack of useful tools that needed fixing, axes and hoe blades and mattocks and rakes, their broken handles made of hand-shaped ash. I collected some delicious new words: *clevis, peen, zerk.*

Two small buildings were beyond repair, their floors rotted through in places. One had been the farm office, and it sat over a basement that had filled with water, visible through a hole in the floor. The other had been used as housing for the hired man, when the farm had been a dairy. We pulled down the buildings and had the foundations filled in with a backhoe.

The ground froze, and all the junk we hadn't sorted yet froze to it. We lit a fire in the fifty-gallon barrel that served as a woodstove in the machine shop and began organizing the things we'd saved, and the things we'd brought with us. Mark set up his forge in one corner, the tongs, hammers, swages, and punches of various shapes and sizes ranged on a shelf next to his old anvil and a tub full of dusty coal. He began fixing the broken tools there, the sparks and scorched smells flying up from the forge, along with the dull sound of a hammer on soft metal. He taught me the various colors of hot—dark cherry, light straw, peacock—and I learned to hold a glowing piece against the anvil with tongs and strike at it awkwardly, the metal mushing like clay. I liked to watch him work, sweating, hammer falling easily from the hinge of his shoulder, his focus moving between the fire and the anvil.

As soon as we'd cleared space in the west barn, we bought a milk cow. She came from a dairy just two miles down the road from us, the Shields farm, a father-son operation that had survived the bad decades by staying on the small side. I'd been reading books about cows—my bedside table held *The Family Cow* and Juliette de Baïracli Levy's *Complete Herbal Handbook for Farm and Stable*—and was eager to deploy my newfound knowledge in the form of incisive questions. I knew that we weren't shopping for the black-and-white cows. Those were Holsteins—big, high-volume producers. The hegemony of Holstein genetics is so strong today that, if in an ad or in conversation the breed is not mentioned, it is assumed to be Holstein.

All other dairy cows are lumped together as "colored breeds." Among them are the Ayrshires, roan-colored and high-strung; Brown Swiss, large, pretty cows with a reputation for low intelligence; Guernseys, hardy and docile; and Jerseys, small, relatively low-volume producers with milk rich in fat and solids. Most dairies in our area keep a few colored cows in their herd, to raise their milk fat and solids numbers, which brings a premium from the milk plant. The Shieldses milked some Jerseys, and these were the cows we were interested in.

Billy Shields walked us through the free-stall barn. We saw a wing-shouldered old gal with a long, withered udder, a chocolate heifer with a wary expression, and then there was Delia.

She was a small-boned Jersey, sloe-eyed and fawn-colored and pied with big patches of white, like a map of lost continents. Her face was delicately dished, and her ears were soft and ladylike, and she stood a little away from the rest of the herd, her hooves deep in the muck. When Mark touched her udder she bent her head around and regarded him with her tolerant, maternal look. She had given birth to two calves, so she was called a second-calf cow, and she was in the middle of her lactation, pregnant with her third. According to her records she was a good milker, giving forty pounds—a little less than five gallons—of milk per day, which made her a steady, if not spectacular, producer. I checked her parts against what I'd gleaned from my reading. Her udder looked firm and well-connected to her body. Her legs were straight and sound. She was registered and in her prime. The Shieldses would part with her because she was a little too meek for the dairy's herd. The Holsteins towered over her and outweighed her by several hundred pounds, and she tended to get pushed around at the feed bunker.

Delia arrived at our farm the next day in a horse trailer, a rope halter around her head. We led her into the barn and released her into the big box stall we'd prepared for her, bedded thickly with mulch hay. She slowly wandered its perimeter, sniffing at the walls, and then lifted her tail and shat. The dark smell of her manure mingled with the green, fermented smell of cow breath and the dry and dusty smell of the hay, and the old barn that had slept so long without a living thing to shelter was awake again, alive with its purpose.

The first time I milked her, I was almost embarrassed by

the intimacy of it. I'd read the instructions in *The Family Cow*, but was I really supposed to touch those long, leathery teats, tucked privately between Delia's hind legs? There are hormones involved in the letdown of milk, primarily oxytocin, the same one that gives nursing mothers that glazed, drunk look of love. When I washed her udder with warm water Delia looked at me like that, one calm brown eye pinned on me as her lower jaw moved in a circle, chewing cud.

I'd found a homemade four-legged milking stool in a dark corner of the barn, its seat worn as smooth as a piece of driftwood. I settled it next to her and rubbed my hands together to warm them, like a gynecologist would. The heat coming from her udder was electric, and the white hairs on the udder reminded me of the soft fuzz on a lady's cheek. I wrapped my hand around a plump teat, pinning the top of it between my thumb and forefinger, and closed each finger in turn until I had the empty teat in my fist. The milk squirted out in an uneven stream, dribbled down my wrist, and soaked into the sleeve of my jacket, as though magnetically repelled by the bucket between my feet. Delia stood with the patience of a large rock, chewing her cud. By the third day of milking the sleeve of my jacket smelled like something that had curled up and died in a warm hole. By the fifth day, my fingers had learned the dance steps, and the milk was hitting the bottom of the bucket with a rhythmic hiss, but my hands cramped into little, arthritic claws before I'd even finished milking the front teats. Then the effects of Delia's letdown reflex would wear off, and no matter how much I squeezed at her the milk would come only in little drips and I'd send her back to her stall with her udder still half full, teats chapped from all my yanking. It was a month before I could milk her reasonably well, the milk flowing into the bucket fast enough to form foam on top. By then my engagement ring no longer fit and my forearms had taken on the heavy look of those of a sailor.

Milking became a kind of physical meditation. It was never easy, and it wasn't always pleasant, but it was rhythmic, predictable, gentle, and quiet. Mark milked in the evening, and I milked in the morning, arriving at the barn in that holy gap between true dark and first light. The electricity in the barn was not working, so I tried to train myself to work by feel until one morning I reached blind and bare-handed into the grain bin and a mouse ran over my hand. I found a lantern and hung it from a beam, and the bats, on the way home from their night shift, flitted in and out of its soft light. By the time I had finished with Delia, the sun was fully up, and they'd squeezed into their resting places between the rafters, above the nests that the swallows would fill with chicks in the spring.

Milking wasn't half the job. The milk in the bucket contained tiny flecks of dirt, cow hairs, and sloughed-off dry skin from the udder and teat. We didn't have a proper milk strainer, so we filtered the milk through an old T-shirt tied with a bungee cord to a stainless-steel funnel. We didn't have a cream separator, either, so when we wanted cream we'd let the milk sit in a tank Mark had rigged up in the barn. It had a valve in the bottom made from the cutoff tip of a water bottle stuck on a clear plastic tube, and after the cream had risen to the top of the tank we'd let the skim milk run out into a bucket until we could see the cream through the tube, then switch buckets to catch the cream. Then we'd stack all the dirty equipment in the front seat of the car and haul it back to the house in town for washing in a sink the size of a postage stamp. It was a very awkward system.

Somehow, we got through those first weeks of milking without giving Delia mastitis—an infected milk duct, scourge of all lactating mamas—or making ourselves sick. I learned to make butter by shaking cream in a gallon jar until lumps formed, bright yellow islands in a sea of foamy white. I bought books on cheese making, and a bottle of rennet. When Mark brought home the evening milk, I'd pick out an interesting recipe and experiment. My first attempts were simple cottage cheeses, just a few drops of rennet stirred into the still-warm milk. Twenty minutes later, through some mysterious alchemical process, the milk would be solid enough to cut into cubes. The pale yellow whey would seep from the cubes of curd, and I'd gently heat it, drawing out more whey, until the curd had shrunk and become firm. Then I'd spoon the curd into a cheesecloth, salt it, and let it drain, and we'd have enough cottage cheese to last us a week. Once I was confident with cottage cheese I expanded my repertoire. I made a few balls of provolone and hung them behind the cellar door to age, but they were so delicious we ate them young.

The farmhouse was split into two apartments, which had been rented out cheaply to a succession of young tenants. Inside, it smelled of pot and Raid. The downstairs was occupied by a quiet, pale couple who looked enough alike to be siblings and couldn't have been long out of high school. Lisa smoked long, thin cigarettes and kept the apartment very tidy and clean. Troy had a collection of miniature John Deere tractors and toy farm implements arranged along the windowsills and across the coffee table, and a John Deere welcome mat guarded the stairs to the cellar. Troy came from a farming family that no longer had a farm. He worked on a construction crew and helped out part-time with milking at the Shieldses' dairy down the road. The year before, he told us, he'd considered getting back into farming in a small way, by raising some replacement heifers in his spare time. He'd gone as far as to clear space for them in the west barn, but a relative had talked him out of it, convincing him it was too risky, a losing proposition.

Troy's story and the little toy tractors reminded me of all the rural places we'd seen in our search for land, the unused farms on good soil, the empty silos jutting up into the horizon, and the generations of accumulated skill and local knowledge and the sense of belonging to a place that would dead-end with this generation. I'd begun to think that the prevailing explanation for what was happening to farms—young people just don't want to work so hard anymore—was a lie. The forces were bigger than that. It was decades of misbegotten farm policy and ag schools and extension agents telling farmers to get bigger, milk harder, plant from hedgerow to hedgerow. It was the consequent supersizing of machinery and debt. It was the enormous weight of that debt against a shrinking milk check, numbers that didn't add up, no matter how hard or long you worked. It was the bad wet year that finished you off, the cows sold at auction, the wildness creeping back into the bank-owned fields, poplar first, and scrubby cedar. It was the barn roof beginning to sag, and nobody there to buttress it. It was the house you grew up in, empty, that attracted the bored and horny young, who broke its windows, had sex on the derelict couch, left their initials and the date scribbled on the once-scrubbed walls. If you are a young man driving by places like that on your way to a steady if low-paying job, no wonder you're easily convinced that farming is a losing proposition, and the only thing left of your rightful legacy is a row of toy tractors, which have not put you into much debt.

The upstairs apartment was rented to a guy in his twenties named Roy Reynolds. He had short-cropped hair and a sparse beard, grown long. His neck was so meaty that it pushed the skin of his scalp upward, making abstract crenulations across the back of his head. His eyelids were weighted down with pads of fat, and he had a habit of tipping his head back and crossing his arms when he talked to you so you couldn't tell if he was glaring or simply regarding you. Outside, in all weather, he wore a thin white undershirt that left an inch of belly above the belt exposed. When the temperature dipped below freezing he added a tall, faux fur hat, hot pink, which somehow made him look more menacing instead of less.

Roy had been running his own dairy farm until the year before. He'd been ambitious and he'd gotten fairly big very fast, financed by a wealthy partner. Roy told us that he'd been milking three hundred Holsteins when he and the partner had a falling-out, and when the partner pulled out Roy had found himself deeply in debt. "They repoed my farm," he told us. If there was any sadness in him it was hidden behind a bright kind of toughness. "I have never woken up in the dark and thought, Dang, I wish I could go milk three hundred cows right now," he said. Since the bankruptcy, he'd been making a living as a truck driver.

If any of the tenants resented us for getting them kicked out of their house as soon as the lease was up, the only one who showed it was the pit bull, Duke. When we walked past on the way to the barns he leered at us from the doghouse, and occasionally he'd make another silent run at us, full speed into the end of his chain. He belonged to Lisa and Troy, and with them he was kittenish, lolling on his back, begging for a scratch on the chest. Roy owned the two cringing white dogs. They were strays he'd picked up at a truck stop, and he'd named the male dog Turbo and the female Fried. They lived loose outside all year, wandering the roads, returning to eat from the fifty-pound bag of kibble Roy left ripped open for them in the garage, an arrangement that made the rats as content as the dogs.

It was Roy who pulled up to our rental house in town on a cold, overcast day and told us we needed to call a vet. "Something happened to your milk cow," he said heavily. "My dogs had something to do with it."

We'd built a little corral off of Delia's stall, so that she could go outside during the day if she wanted to, and that's where we found her, standing still, her head drooping nearly to the ground. Her soft ears were tattered, bloody ribbons hanging limp next to her head. Her eyes were swollen almost shut, and the blood from two dozen wounds dripped from her face onto the frozen ground. Her udder was cut, and she had lacerations on her belly and each of her legs. I couldn't believe an animal could be so injured and still standing. It was painful to look at her.

Duke had gotten loose. Nobody had ever heard of a dog attacking a healthy cow in broad daylight, but that's what happened. In my imagination, I see him finding her alone in her corral, circling her, Delia lowering her hornless, defenseless head, and Duke snapping at her nose, drawing blood. Then the white dogs joining in, goaded by the smell of blood and the frenzied Duke and the lowing of the suffering cow. By the time Roy and Troy heard the commotion, all three dogs were slick with blood.

The vet, David Goldwasser, a slight and gentle man who moved deliberately and looked tired, arrived. I thought he would advise us to put Delia down, but he said that of all the large animals cows are the most resilient, and he thought she would probably pull through. It was good that it was cold, because there was less risk of infection, and she would not be tormented by flies. He clipped the hair from around her wounds and dressed and sewed up the worst of them. Her ears were beyond repair, so he took out some scissors and cut them away, leaving a pair of raw and waxy nubbins that stood out from the sides of her head like the hard blooms of some strange tropical plant. She stood placidly for him, wondering mutely at her own pain, and when we had to milk her full udder that evening, trying to be as gentle as possible with the injured tissue, she never raised a hoof at us.

They shot all three dogs. The next spring, when the snow melted, I found their collars in the mud next to the garage. Such is the way of rural people, no clemency. What if it had been a kid, they said. For Roy Reynolds it was the unsentimental last straw in a series of aggravations those white dogs had caused him, but Troy must have loved that big brute of a pit. When we knocked on his door to collect a check for the vet bill, which all three of them had offered to pay, he was red-eyed.

The town of Essex, sleepy with the approach of winter, had detected the presence of newcomers and roused itself to greet us. In one week, two people knocked on the door of our rental house bearing actual welcome baskets, and three others came by to invite us to the Tuesday-night potluck at St. John's Episcopal Church. I didn't know what to make of such friendliness. In the city, the only reason neighbors knocked on your door was to complain about the noise you were making. It occurred to me that there is more distance between rural and the urban in the same country—the same state!—than there is between cities on different continents. I would have felt more at home in Istanbul, Rome, or Yangon. Here, I was a true foreigner, making it up as I went along.

There were seven hundred people living in town, and everyone we met already knew our backstory with varying degrees of accuracy, and they all knew the farm better than we did. "How's your tree spade working?" Dave Lansing, the fire chief, asked us. We had no idea. "I hear it's broken," he said. We were visited by the town's doyenne, an elegant woman who went by the disarming name of Frisky. She invited us to her house for dinner, which began with sherry and ended with poached pears and for which we were underdressed. The next week we met some people our age who had us to dinner at the off-the-grid cabin they'd built themselves, set into the woods a few miles outside of town. They made a party of it, inviting other young couples, and after dinner the babies were laid down to sleep on the bed and the fiddles came out and the cabin filled up with music, like an episode of *Little House on the Prairie,* but with beer.

Every day, people drove into the farm to introduce themselves and to satisfy their curiosity. They'd heard the outline of our plans, and wanted to judge for themselves whether or not the situation was as hopeless as it sounded. We'd installed a proper woodstove in one of the newer outbuildings, a small, well-insulated cabin that Lars had built for his caretaker to use as an office. A few sticks of wood kept it warm all day, and in cold weather we ate lunch in there, and received guests. One day I returned from some errand to find Mark sitting with Neal Owens, a man so big he dwarfed the furniture and the room. His great size was counterbalanced by an aura of diffidence and humble courtesy. He had heard we were interested in draft horses, and he'd brought some equipment that had been sitting around his place too long, some good-looking collars and pieces of harness that he said we could borrow.

His family had been in the neighborhood so long that a road to our south was named for them; the farm his father and grandfather had grown up on was just over the next hill, but it had been sold out of the family. There were farmers in each generation, and Neal and his brother, Donald, had run a dairy, too, until a combination of debt and bad luck had bankrupted them. They'd been in their twenties then. Now they had kids of their own, three boys between them, and Neal and Donald and Neal's wife, Tammy, and the kids and their grandparents all lived together in a rented house. Tammy worked two jobs, and Neal managed the kids and worked part-time, putting together the county fair and also serving as town dogcatcher. The house they rented came with a barn and some pasture, and the kids kept an ever-shifting collection of goats, dogs, calves, ponies, rabbits, chickens, and geese, which, to hear Neal tell it, they traded like other kids trade baseball cards: a billy goat for five rabbits, or all the chickens sold at auction in order to buy a calf for a 4-H project.

Before Neal left that day, we'd struck a tentative deal for his family to make our hay the next year. Neal and Donald had made hay since they were kids and knew the equipment. Their dad, a hale seventy-something, would help out. They'd use our tractors and our land, and we'd buy the hay back from them at a reduced price.

Shane Sharpe and Bud Campbell came by to meet us one afternoon, too, on one of their weekend tours around the neighborhood. Shane's son Luke, a husky teenager with Down syndrome, was sandwiched between them in the cab. Shane and Bud kept their cooler of Busch in the back of Shane's pickup, accessible for the conversations that took place at each stop, while they stood leaning into the truck bed. Shane owned a machine shop that made parts for the defense industry, and it had done well enough that he'd retired from the day-to-day work of it by the time he turned forty. He was known locally as a mechanical genius, the kind of guy who can walk into our shop, where Mark has been muttering and torquing away for hours with some tool I don't even know the name of, take one look at the situation, and then make a small and profound suggestion that lifts the veil of confusion to reveal a simple, elegant solution. Since retirement he'd spent his time fooling around with his sawmill or his draft horses or doing favors for friends who needed something fixed, and, if nothing else was going on, you could find him in his shop, patiently restoring a 1939 Dodge flatbed truck that he was planning to paint candy apple red. Shane was the only person I'd ever met outside of literature who suffered from gout. His doctors had told him the gout would get better if he quit drinking, and occasionally he made short feints in that direction. Bud, who was a carpenter and lived alone, did not pretend to want to quit.

It was Shane who dispelled the rumor that had been circulating around Dale Ranger's barn in the valley west of ours. Dale tolerates drinking at evening milking, so he is rarely short of help. I think it started because at the time I was still wearing the standard-issue city clothes that I'd moved with, tailored shirts and skirts cut above the knee and boots with a little bit of heel, and this is a town where lip gloss is considered daring, a special-occasion accessory. Someone decided I was formerly a high-end prostitute in New York City, and this news was fully believed and widely disseminated by the men at Dale's barn until Shane got to know us and reported back that I was not an ex-whore after all and had graduated from college, to which, Shane said, Bud Campbell had replied, *I don't know, it's just what I heard.*

We also got to know Thomas LaFountain, a tall and heav-

ily built man with twinkly blue eyes who runs the local cus-
tom butcher shop, where hunters take their deer to be cut and
packaged in the fall. Thomas told us he'd been a heavy drinker
and a dangerous barroom brawler before his doctor and his
wife ganged up on him, told him he'd have to quit or die alone,
and so he quit, at once and for good.

For a long time, Thomas and Shane were the only men
who talked directly to me. The rest of them would pull in, roll
down the truck window, and ask, "Mark around?" or "'Stha
boss here?" and then would sit silently until Mark appeared,
directing all questions, comments, and dealings to him and
ignoring me completely. When departing, they'd say, "See you
later, Mark," even if I'd been standing there the entire time,
trying to interject my opinion. Mark is so much taller than I
am, nobody even made eye contact with me. But then Thomas
or Shane would come by when Mark happened to be gone,
and actually acknowledge my existence, and instead of leaving immediately they'd roll down their truck windows to chat,
and I would suddenly realize that I had no idea what to say to
them, no subject at disposal that seemed of common interest,
and I would get nervous and say whatever weird things came
into my head just to fill up the silence. Both of them handled
my awkwardness with courtesy.

It took me the better part of a year to figure out that here,
talking doesn't necessarily have to have a point. It really *can*
be about the weather, or it can comfortably tread over already
well-covered ground. In fact, it's perfectly acceptable to not
talk at all. I learned this while hanging around Thomas's shop,
wrapping cuts of pork that he'd butchered for us. It was deer

season, and Thomas was busy, working well into the evening, the cooler full of field-dressed carcasses, a pile of venison ribs growing into a tall heap outside the door. Poop Henderson, a man in his fifties with a gray beard long enough to tuck into the front of his pants and black-framed glasses with thick and cloudy lenses, came in. Poop lives with his mother and rarely leaves the valley, traveling in a triangle from his house to Thomas's butcher shop to Dale's barn with a pair of Busch cans tucked into his shirt pockets. Poop and Thomas exchanged monosyllabic greetings, and Poop extracted one of his beers from its pocket and took a seat next to the meat saw as Thomas boned a shoulder of venison, measured his sausage spices, the salt and pepper and sage, and ran the seasoned meat through the grinder, the local country station playing softly in the background. They did not say a word until an hour later when Poop lifted himself up, said, "Well, I suppose," which was answered by "All right," and exited. That counted as a visit, and it is what friends and neighbors do.

The people we met kept telling us, with varying degrees of tact, that we'd fail. They said nobody in the area was interested in local or organic food, or even if they were interested, they wouldn't be able to afford it. And if we did find people to buy our food we'd still fail, because the farm was too wet and nothing would grow. And if we managed to grow something *and* sell it, well, then, it was only a matter of time before we'd fail, farming being farming. Some people said these things aloud to us, and others intimated them, and either way I'd feel a little jangle of anxiety that I would try to suppress until Mark and I were alone. I had no expertise in what we were doing, and no perspective on whether I should trust in Mark's optimism or the general pessimism. If we did fail, I had no plan B. It was not like I could just walk back into my old life. I no longer had an apartment, for one, and I wouldn't have the money for a deposit, since we were spending everything we had on things like cows. Once, an elderly neighbor, Trudy, came over with a box of extra pots and pans and gadgets she'd gleaned from her kitchen. They were good enameled cast-iron pots, and we accepted them gratefully. Later, another neighbor came by and asked if Trudy had brought us the pots and pans. "She thought you were poor!" he said, cheerfully. "She thought you were, you know, needy. I tried to explain to her that you're needy *by choice.*" That exchange depressed me for days. I kept seeing the kids in my grade school who were labeled "needy," kids with drawn faces and crusty snot mustaches and clothes that didn't seem fresh, and I'd look in the mirror and compare.

When we would talk about our future in private, I would ask Mark if he really thought we had a chance. Of course we had a chance, he'd say, and anyway, it didn't matter if this venture failed. In his view, we were already a success, because we were doing something hard and it was something that mattered to us. You don't measure things like that with words like *success* or *failure,* he said. Satisfaction comes from trying hard things and then going on to the next hard thing, regardless of the outcome. What mattered was whether or not you were moving in a direction you thought was right. This sounded extremely fishy to me.

This conversation played out many times, with me anxious, Mark calm, until once, as we sat together reviewing our expenses, I was almost in tears. I felt like we were teetering over an abyss. I wasn't asking him to guarantee that we'd be rich. I just wanted him to assure me that we'd be solvent, that we'd be, as I put it, okay. Mark laughed. "What is the worst thing that could happen?" he asked. "We're smart and capable people. We live in the richest country in the world. There is food and shelter and kindness to spare. What in the world is there to be afraid of?"

He traced this opinion of his to a very specific moment. He was twenty-one years old and had just graduated from Swarthmore with a degree in agricultural science, a major they did not offer but one he'd put together for himself out of classes in biology, chemistry, and economics. He wanted to see what farming was like across America, and to see what rural life was like, and he wanted to see it up close. He set off from his parents' house in New Paltz, his bicycle loaded down with a tent and a change of clothes, and rode west. It was summer, and he told his grandmother he'd spend Christmas with her at her home in California.

He took very little money with him, partly because he had very little money at the time and partly because he had a sense that money would insulate him from his adventure. The first week of his trip he rode two days through a difficult patch of construction in New Jersey, feeling frazzled by the noise of trucks and by the heat bouncing off the asphalt. Late one afternoon he saw a biker coming toward him on the other side of the road, loaded down with gear that looked a lot like his.

His name was Carl and he'd come from Seattle, biking the same route that Mark was just setting out on, but in the opposite direction. Carl told Mark what an awful trip he was about to have, what an awful country America was, rife with mean-spirited people and patrolled by bully cops who were just looking for an excuse to give you trouble. Then they went their separate ways, Carl pointed east, with Mark's parents' address in his pocket, and Mark pointed west.

Mark made it across the border into Pennsylvania that day, and by evening he was in a little town on the Delaware River. He looked for a place to camp—wary now, and on the lookout for cops. He saw a park with a basketball court, where two young dads were shooting hoops, their toddlers playing in the grass. Mark asked if they thought he could camp there, and they said they didn't see why not. He pitched his tent next to a copse of trees, and he was among the shadows of those trees stripping off his clothes to wash himself down with a quart of water he carried for that purpose when he looked up to see a man walking toward him, carrying something. Mark is nearsighted, and his first thought was that it was a cop, and there he was naked in the shadows with toddlers in the vicinity, and he was probably going to get arrested and charged as a sex offender. By the time he had his pants on he could see that it was not a cop but one of the dads who had been shooting hoops and he was carrying a plate loaded with fried chicken and sweet corn, and a big glass of iced tea. "Thought you might be hungry," the dad said.

The rest of the trip was exactly like that, full of good people offering food and shelter and kindness, genuine kindness. At the end of his day of travel Mark would look for a certain type of farm, one with a garden, not too big and not too polished, but in good repair, without the whiff of desperation. He'd knock on a farmhouse door and ask if it would be all right to camp somewhere on their place. He was never refused, not once. Nine times out of ten the door would open and the next thing he knew he'd be saying grace with a family at their dinner table, and soon after that he'd find himself tucked into a bed in the guest room. He'd often spend a day or two working on the place, and in this way he saw all sorts of different farms and met all kinds of farm families. He saw feed lots and citrus plantations. He hoed beans on a small-scale organic vegetable farm and rode a combine through a thousand acres of corn, the corn pouring out of the machine like a smooth gold river. He stopped to get maps at a Chamber of Commerce in the middle of the country, and the man at the desk went out to his car and came back with a pack of new socks. "Here," he said. "You always need good socks on a trip like this." He stayed four or five days with a family that grew corn and beans in Indiana; the wife, Connie, ran a beauty salon, and after Mark was fed and rested she took him into town and sat him in her chair and washed his hair, twice, because the water was still brown after the first washing, and then she gave him a haircut. Connie still sends him Christmas cards, pictures of her grandkids tucked inside. I'd seen them, so I knew it was true.

That story became the counterbalance to my anxiety. That, plus the one dissenting voice in the neighborhood. Shep Shields lived just over the hill from us and had been farming all his life. He was a short figure on legs so insulted by decades of labor they hardly bent at the knee at all. He propelled himself with a kind of side-to-side motion that made him look like a mechanical toy. His hand, on the end of his walking stick, was knotted up with arthritis, and he still fed a herd of beef cattle every morning. He told me he loved draft horses, dogs, and pretty women, not necessarily in that order. He blamed the state of his body on the fact that he'd worked too hard as a child, hefting ninety-pound milk cans onto a truck from the age of ten. When he heard our plan, he didn't say he thought we'd fail. He didn't say we'd succeed, either, but he gave us a nod of encouragement and told us we were on the right track. He'd seen eighty years of change in agriculture, the arrival of the tractor, the milking machine, the bulk tank, all the chemicals and medications and devices that grease the gears of large-scale farming, and he'd thought about all these things, and seen their effects. If he were a young man just starting out, he said, he'd do it with horses again, and keep it simple and small, grow things you can eat, with maybe a handful of good Jersey cows, milked for butter or cheese. Keep it local. Feed yourselves, feed your neighbors, the way it had been done when he was a boy.

The days turned so cold the snow went squeaky, and heavy steam rose every morning from the channel the ferry kept open on the lake. Inside our cold house, the frost line in the basement sank deeper every day. We wrapped the pipes in heat tape and kept the woodstove stoked, but it warmed only a shockingly small circle directly in front of it. For a week, the thermometer on the outside of the house never broke into double digits. At the farm, the hens' combs went black with frostbite, and the "frost-free" hydrant froze solid. We hauled water in buckets from the pump house, careful to keep our hands dry. I learned the weight of water, a little more than eight pounds per gallon, forty pounds per bucket, eighty pounds for every full and balanced load, the handles cutting deeply into my hands despite my thick gloves, my shoulders thickening and rounding with new muscle.

The farm was locked down with the cold. It had been years since I'd experienced a real winter, and I couldn't stay warm, no matter what I wore. My feet became insensible blocks and my hands ached. Between milkings and chores we retreated to the house in town, shedding our stiff clothes at the door, and eagerly stoked the fire. The bed was beyond the comfort of the woodstove's heat, and in the morning I'd vault from under the covers to the woodstove, clothes in hand, wincing at every step on the freezing floor. Mark read *East of Eden* to me at night before we went to sleep, tucked under three blankets, wearing thick hats and wool socks.

There was plenty of work to be done indoors. We needed to tap into the local farmer network, because, despite their reputation for independence, farmers are by necessity interconnected, exchanging among themselves labor, machinery, expertise, commodities, and information. Along with his tools and his tractors, Mark had left behind in Pennsylvania all the friendly connections he'd built with his neighbor farmers, the kinds that are vital when you need a part welded during harvest season or when you run out of hay at the end of winter and need a decent price on bales to get you through to spring. As with all else, here we'd be starting from scratch. Mark spent long hours on the phone, making contacts, arranging visits.

At the same time, we were looking for a team of horses. Mark called his Amish friends in Pennsylvania for advice. They told us we wanted a specific sort of team, calm and easy-going, well-broke to all kinds of farm machinery, horses who had seen a lot of work but still had a few good years in them. Geldings would be preferable to mares, all other things being equal.

There are two kinds of trouble in a search for a team like this. First is scarcity. The market for draft horses is small and specialized and not nearly as rich as it is for light horses. Whatever money there is in drafts is in the showy end, the kinds of horses you see hitched to wagons in parades and at county fairs, or the massive horses you see at horse pulls, where teams compete to drag enormous weights over short distances. Breeders produce the type of horse they can sell, so most horses on the market fit one of those two types. The former are leggy, high-headed, high-stepping, flashy horses with a lot of nervous energy. The latter are muscular and explosively powerful, but they tend to be ill-broke and physically damaged, and are not always well-treated, a combination that makes them unpredictable and potentially dangerous.

Calm, experienced, healthy drafts were scarce, and almost never for sale. An Amishman or a serious horse farmer who wants "using horses" will make them, not buy them, and if he makes a good one, he'll hold on to it, and use it for as long as possible. If a horse like this is for sale, it's usually because there is something wrong with it—an unstable temperament or poor health.

A few dozen phone calls had rendered one promising lead, a dealer across the lake from us. We took the ferry to Vermont and drove to the Coopers' farm. They ran a large dairy, but they'd always dealt in horses and had a reputation for integrity, a rare trait in horse traders.

It was snowing when we pulled up to the Coopers' farmhouse, a low ranch on a dirt road that was overshadowed by the long red barn next to it. Jim Cooper came out to greet us in plain clothes, flat hat, and those curious Mennonite whiskers. He walked us into his barn, which was full of the biggest horses I'd ever seen, their muscular haunches protruding from straight stalls into the central aisle, black, brown, and roan, all of them higher than my head.

His son, in his early twenties, had a colt in the crossties, a Percheron, well-built and fit with a black hide that shone like a pair of new boots. He was wearing a bridle over his halter, and the lines were buckled into a bitting rig, a strap of leather that encircled his barrel. The horse mouthed the bit, chomping up and down, ears half back, not nervous but not completely at ease. Jim's son unsnapped the crossties and led the colt past us, to the paddock where a few horses were loafing. Jim explained that this was the way he started his young horses, by turning them out in a bitting rig and letting them get used to it on their own time, in the comforting presence of their herd mates.

Then Jim's son backed a fleshy roan mare out of one of the straight stalls at the end of the aisle, and Jim brought out her mate, another mare, so well-matched I had to look for ways to tell them apart. They were Belgians, eight years old, well-broke, Jim said, and well-mannered. "But horses are horses," he said, "and there's no such thing as bombproof." He and his son went over them with brushes, lifted the collars over their heads and settled them on their shoulders, all their movements spare and calm in that horseman's way of hurrying that keeps the horses at ease. "Had a man once," he said, "who wanted to get into drafts. His wife was nervous about horses, so he wanted a bombproof team." He pulled a heavy leather harness from its hook next to the mare's stall. "I had a pair of geldings to show them. A real steady team. Kind of horses a child or a woman could drive." He hefted the hames above his head and settled them gently into the groove of the collar, and laid the rest of the harness along the mare's back, where it balanced in an incomprehensible tangle while he stepped in front of the mare to buckle the hame strap. "Man came out to see the team. These were good horses." He walked behind the mare and pulled the harness over her haunches, the tangle of leather falling neatly into place. He pulled her bobbed tail over the britchen and then buckled the bellyband. "Hitched them up to the wagon and we started across the road." He had a bridle by the headstall. The mare dropped her nose, and he slipped the bridle over her head, buckled the throatlatch, and hooked the curb chain under her chin. Jim's son had the other mare harnessed, and he brought her up next to her mate and they buckled the lines to the bits. "Got to the other side of the road and a bee stung one of the geldings and off they went at a run. Man got so scared he jumped off the back of the wagon. Hit his head on the edge of it and died. Just like that. These were good horses, never gave me any trouble. Yep. No such thing as bombproof. Step up, mare."

The snow had stopped falling, and the air had turned sharply colder. The wind picked up the new snow and blew it in twists across the open field. The mares seemed to take on its nervous energy and pulled at their bits. Jim stepped the near horse over the pole of a heavily built sled that was waiting in the driveway, and his son snapped the neck yoke to the harnesses, placed the pole in its ring, and then hooked the tug chains to the evener. Jim had the lines in his hand, and when we were all settled in the sled he spoke to the horses and they stepped out eagerly. The driveway was icy, and the mares scrabbled to keep their feet.

Across the road, the field was deep in snow, and the mares had to work to break a trail. Jim whoaed them, and they danced in place, pulling hard at their bits. "Drop that mare down," he told his son, who jumped off the sled and waded to the off mare's head. He unbuckled the lines from the ring of her bit and rebuckled them halfway down the bit's arms. I knew from riding horses that this would give Jim the leverage to pressure the mare's tongue and bars between the bit and the curb chain. I looked at Jim's sturdy frame and wondered how in the world I would be able to control this much horse. We struck out again, but the mares didn't settle. Instead of a walk, they minced along at a nervous trot. "They haven't been worked since fall," Jim explained. "If you wanted them, I'd work them for you every day for a couple weeks, get them sharp." And then, after a few more minutes of struggle, he whoaed again, exhaled, and said, "You don't want these horses. Go see Gary Duquette. He's got a team for sale that he bought from me a few years back. They'll be what you're looking for."

And they were. The team was hitched when we arrived, an eight-year-old boy neighbor of Gary's up on the wagon like a bowsprit, holding the lines. It was a hardscrabble hillside farm, a few cattle lipping silage behind a single strand of high-tensile wire. Gary was in the listing barn, tending to a tiny calf that was sick with pneumonia, gaunt-sided and struggling for breath. He said with regret he'd have to take it behind the barn and shoot it later on. We mounted the wagon, and he spoke to the horses, and they set off at an easy walk. Half a mile along the frozen dirt road, Gary said, "You gonna buy 'em, you might as well drive 'em," and I took lines in my hands for the first time. It was like holding live things, a pair of tame snakes. Riding, you have your whole body—heels, legs, seat, weight, and hands—in communication with the horse. Moreover, you're on top, a position of power. When you're driving a team, all that communication—the whole intense conversation—takes place through a few inches of leather running across your palms, your connection to the horses' mouths. And there are two of them, blind to everything but the road in front of them. And they weigh a ton each. And you are strapped to them from behind, your fates bound. I guess I'd imagined draft horses would be boring compared to the horses I liked to ride—the hot, wild type that will move off your heel like drag racers—but I glimpsed that day how wrong I was.

Sam and Silver arrived at the farm two weeks later. Mark and I had spent the week banging together a pair of straight stalls for them in the west barn, the bitter cold sending shock waves to the elbow with every whack of the hammer. We spread a thick layer of straw in the stalls and filled the new mangers with hay, and we were ready. They stepped off the trailer like kings. That such creatures exist moves me. That they labor for us, willingly and with heart, is miraculous.

They were Belgian geldings, sorrel-colored, with flaxen manes and tails. Their histories were murky, but they were supposed to be fourteen years old, used for farm work, parades, and pulling, bought separately at auction and paired up by Jim Cooper. Silver was the looker of the two. The vast majority of male horses are castrated when they're young, to prevent unintended breedings and make them more tractable. Gary told us Silver had been a breeding stallion until he was past ten years old. He still had a typical stallion's neck, thick, arched, and heavily muscled. He looked custom-built for pulling heavy things, with a wide chest, well-sprung ribs, and a short back. His expression was powerful and confident if not stunningly intelligent. Sam was his opposite, angular, stringy, and wise. His action was snappier, and he carried himself like an enlisted soldier, upright and a little tense. Sam's ear flicked back when you spoke to him, and he conveyed the sense, like some horses do, that he would do his best to take care of you, even if you did something stupid. They both topped eighteen hands, so tall I had to stand on a bucket to brush their backs.

The next morning after milking, I backed Silver out of his stall and put his bridle on, climbed a stack of hay bales, and leapt onto his bare back. It was like riding a warm sofa. When he moved, it was an oceanic roll. He seemed a little bewildered at the strange, small weight on his back, the unfamiliar feeling of legs wrapped around him, and it occurred to me that he'd probably never been ridden before. I put him back and bridled Sam, whose sharp withers were not nearly as comfortable as Silver's broad back. But Sam was eager to go. We rode out through snowdrifts to the big rise at the eastern edge of the farm. From the rise, there is a good view of the lake, and the wind had blown the frozen ground free from snow. I gave Sam a little kick, and he set off at a canter, stretching his long legs, his huge stride eating ground. I felt a familiar joy pulse through me, the feeling horses have given me since childhood. Sam seemed willing to run for miles, but I was a little worried, at that speed, that I might lose my seat on his bare back and crash. I pulled him back down to a walk, smiling. He might be a plow horse, I thought, but he's got a Thoroughbred soul.

Mark came home late one frozen Sunday carrying a bag of small, silver fish. They were smelts, locally known as icefish. He'd bought them at the store in the next town south, across from which a little village had sprung up on the ice of the lake, a collection of shacks with holes drilled in and around them. I'd seen the men going from the shore to the shacks on snowmobiles, six-packs of beer strapped on behind them like a half-dozen miniature passengers. "Sit and rest," Mark said. "I'm cooking." He sautéed minced onion in our homemade butter, added a little handful of crushed, dried sage, and when the onion was translucent, he sprinkled in flour to make a roux, which he loosened with beer, in honor of the fishermen. He added cubed carrot, celery root, potato, and some stock, and then the fish, cut into pieces, and when they were all cooked through he poured in a whole morning milking's worth of Delia's yellow cream. Icefish chowder, rich and warm, eaten while sitting in Mark's lap, my feet so close to the woodstove that steam came off my damp socks.

As we were scraping the bottoms of our bowls, Mark pulled out a piece of paper covered in hieroglyphics, words and arrows and cryptic symbols. At first I thought it was his latest plan for the farm, but then I picked out familiar names. It was a guest list. For our wedding. "Oh," I said and slipped off his lap. "We *are* engaged, you know," he said, not quite looking at me. "Yep," I said. "I'm aware." I was dug in by then, more and more each day, but a nervous little animal inside of me had begun squirreling around, looking for an exit. The deeper my commitment, the more desperate that animal became. In love, and in most other parts of my life, my pattern had always been to be a tourist, not a citizen. I would dive in deep but soon get out of the pool. I was not insincere. I always truly believed. It's just that, on personality tests, I score dizzyingly high on novelty-seeking behavior. The word *forever* just plain scares me. I was completely enthralled with the farm. I was passionately in love with Mark. But knowing myself, I really, really didn't know if either love could last.

We had tentatively agreed that the wedding should take place in the fall, after harvest, at the farm. In early October the food would be plentiful but the weather still fine. It had seemed so far off, but now it was less than a year away, almost close enough to see. "Hey, maybe we should wait until *next* fall," I said, trying to make it sound light, as though it had just occurred to me. "What with everything we have to do and all." We'd been engaged for a year already, and he'd wanted to get married right away. He stood up, bowl in hand, and headed for the sink. "I'm not waiting another year," he said from the kitchen. "If you don't want to get married this fall, I don't want to get married at all."

There is no better lesson in commitment than the cow. Her udder knows no exceptions or excuses. She must be milked, or she'll suffer from her own fullness, and then she'll get sick or dry up. Morning and evening, on holidays, in good weather and in bad, from the day she gives birth to her calf until the day ten months later when you dry her off, your cow is the frame in which you must fit your days, the twelve-hour tether beyond which you may no longer travel. What she gives you in exchange for your commitment is impressive. She is the cornerstone of the farm, the great converter. She takes grass—that ubiquitous terrestrial plankton—and uses the four-part trick of rumination to unlock its cellulose, release its energy. There's a liturgical sound to our names for her stomachs—*omasum, abomasum, reticulum*—and in old words for these parts, you can hear a certain reverence: *king's-hood,* the second stomach, and *psalterium,* the third. The word *cream* is related to the word *chrism,* to anoint. Royal words, holy words, for a very humble process. It makes sense, though, when you consider that from the cow comes a whole farmstead of abundance. Milk, cheese, butter, yogurt, cream, and the by-products—skim milk, buttermilk, whey—to fatten your pigs and feed your poultry. And she gives you a calf every year, which you can raise (on grass again), for a year's worth of beef for a family. All this flows from a cow.

I was getting better at milking, faster, the milk no longer dribbling down my wrists or jetting erratically toward the barn wall. I'd learned to keep my nails short and smooth, and to strip each teat gently but thoroughly. My forearms were bigger every week.

Milk was uncharted territory for me. Aside from the half-and-half I put in my coffee, I hadn't drunk it in years. I was mildly lactose intolerant, and the thought of milk as a beverage kind of grossed me out. But raw milk from a Jersey cow is a totally different substance from what I'd thought of as milk. If you do not own a cow or know someone who owns a cow, I must caution you never to try raw milk straight from the teat of a Jersey cow, because it would be cruel to taste it once and not have access to it again. Only a few people in America remember this type of milk now, elderly people, mostly, who grew up with a cow. They come to the farm sometimes, looking for that taste from their childhood.

Once you're used to farm milk, commercial milk has a lot of drawbacks. First, there is the taste of cardboard and sometimes, faintly, the taste of the chemicals that are used to wash the udder and flush the pipes of the milking machine. There is the homogenization process, the ubiquity of which puzzles me. Why would you *not* want your cream on top of your milk, where it is ready to be sloshed into your coffee in the morning, leaving the now-skimmer milk for drinking purposes? And then there's pasteurization, which changes the taste and nature of milk as much as heat changes any food from raw to cooked.

Fresh raw milk is wonderful, but as it ages, things get really interesting. Milk as it comes from the cow is a warm, sugary, proteinaceous substance, a lively medium for bacterial growth. When the bacteria multiply, they acidify the milk, changing its taste from sweet to tart, eventually thickening it. When you look at old cookbooks that call for "sour milk," this is what they are talking about. If you leave good, clean raw milk from a healthy cow in a warm place, the "wild" bacteria in it will cause it to solidify into something that's always interesting and almost always edible. Humans have been exploiting this property for a very long time, breeding specific strains of bacteria for desirable and predictable qualities. That's how we turn milk into yogurt, kefir, and various types of cheese. Pasteurization kills almost all bacteria in milk, benign and pathogenic alike. Without the "good" bacteria, pasteurized milk is vulnerable to the kinds of putrefying bacteria that make it rot instead of sour.

Another difference comes from the breed of the cow. The milk you get in the store almost certainly came from a Holstein. These are big cows, and in commercial dairies they are bred and fed to maximize production. But as a general rule, as the volume of milk goes up, the amount of fat and solids in the milk goes down. There's an old farmer's joke about the Jersey dairyman who keeps a Holstein in the barn in case the well runs dry, so he'll have something with which to wash the dishes. Jersey milk is richer by far than Holstein milk, with a higher fat content and also a higher percentage of milk solids. Moreover, because the Jersey cow does not completely metabolize the beta carotene in grass, the cream is tinted a pretty, warm, pale yellow. When you make butter from such cream, especially in spring, the color becomes vibrant.

More than breeding there is the issue of feed. The taste of milk is directly influenced by what a cow is eating. This is most obvious when things go wrong and the cows eat something that gives the milk a taint. Wild garlic in your pasture will give you milk redolent of scampi. Catmint, lamb's-quarter, and goldenrod impart a lobsterish flavor—not terrible in itself but not exactly what you want in a glass of milk. If you feed cows your extra cabbages, you must do it several hours before milking time or your milk will taste like skunk. The texture of the butterfat changes depending on what the cow is eating, too. Butter made from spring milk, when the cows are on lush grass, is soft and easily spreadable. In winter, when the cows are eating hay, the butter is hard and brittle even at room temperature and must be smushed down on a piece of bread instead of spread. There are more subtle effects, too. Milk from a cow grazing a pasture rich in clover tastes different from the same cow's milk when she is in a pasture full of orchard grass, and even the same pasture varies according to season, to weather. Milk, like wine, has a serious *goût de terroir,* characteristics inextricable from the environment in which it is produced. Most commercial milk comes from cows that never step hoof on pasture while they are lactating. Instead of grass they eat what's called a TMR—a total mixed ration. It is carefully calibrated to maximize milk production while minimizing cost and might consist of haylage or silage—chopped, preserved fodder—ground with protein boosters like soy or the malted grain left over from brewing. If you think of milk as a commodity, one squirt pretty much the same as any other, then the TMR makes perfect sense. But if you begin to think of milk as a food with seasonal and regional character, the TMR begins to seem as crazy as making wine out of hydroponic grapes.

Our first blizzard began on a Friday. The weather radio was making grave predictions, but the morning dawned prettily enough, cold, with weak sun filtering through high clouds and a light snow falling straight down. We spent the morning at the farm, battening down the hatches. We locked the chickens in their coop and fired up the tractor, dragging the coop slowly along the driveway to a sheltered spot near the west barn. We locked Delia in her stall, and closed all the barn doors, and headed back to the house in town to wait it out.

We spent the day in a fit of joyful enthusiasm, mapping out the next year of work on a calendar that had come in the mail and was decorated, ironically enough, with a painting of a colonial-style farmhouse, a red barn, and three fluffy white sheep. The lettering read "My Country 'Tis of Thee, Sweet Land of Liberty." We filled in the days and weeks with our ambitions, which even then we must have known were too big to be contained in the boundaries of a single year. The first week in February was reserved to FIGURE OUT GREENHOUSE—BUILD IT! In the second week of that month, we would aim to BUILD DISTRIBUTION AREA and also, somehow, cut and split the next year's FIREWOOD. The day in October when we planned to get married Mark had written WEDDING, and below that, on the same day's square, 50 CHICKS ARRIVE. The letters were the same size, and the only thing that set the first event apart from the second was a pair of conjoined hearts. The following week he had written HONEYMOON and also, neatly, EXTRACT HONEY from the hive.

We got so wrapped up in our plans we failed to notice it had begun to snow in earnest. The sun was low by the time we looked up, and Delia needed milking. Mark was in the middle of making an experimental cheese, waiting for the curd to solidify, so I volunteered to go to the farm to milk for him. It was only a mile, I reasoned. How bad could it be?

I drove at walking pace, hunched over the steering wheel, peering desperately out the window for a glimpse of yellow lines, the only car on the road. Before I'd gone half a mile the road in front of me was dark, and I had to pull warily to the shoulder to wipe a thick pad of snow from the headlights. I got to the barn, and as soon as I turned the wipers off, the windshield went opaque.

Delia was snug enough in her stall, listening to the wind blowing around the corner of the barn. I brought her to her stanchion and milked her, grateful for the warmth of her teats, and put her back home with an extra bale of straw. I watered her and opened her bale of hay, and then went out to catch the horses, who were sheltering in the trees, the snow building up on their backs. By the time they were in their stalls my car was drifted in, so deep I couldn't have used it even if I had been foolish enough to try. I walked in the climax of the storm, feeling like King Lear, face to the wind and mostly blind, through the soughing stand of hemlock, to the road. One truck passed, at a crawl, the sound of it muted by the snow on the ground and the snow so thick in the air that the headlights were useless, little stumpy cones of light. The road disappeared after that, and I had to look for glimpses of the power lines above so as not to lose my way. I arrived home sweating and exhilarated, grateful that the farm and its imperatives had forced me out into the middle of that storm. I imagine that when I am old and immersed in memory I will relive that night and tell the story of it to whoever is around and willing to listen.

The blizzard continued through the night, but by dawn the snow had stopped falling and had begun to blow. We walked back to the farm at milking time on snowshoes, no traffic at all on the road, the setting moon just visible through the clouds. The hemlock branches were weighted almost to the ground, and the snowdrifts were ten feet deep in places. My car was nothing but a wide white hump.

Now that we had the horses we needed equipment for them to pull. We used our snow day to make a list of the tools we would need by spring. First, a plow. All the land that we were planning to use for growing vegetables was covered in thick sod. We would need a plow to turn it, and then more tools—a disc harrow, Mark said, and a spring-tine harrow—to smooth the turned land into a seedbed level enough to plant. Once the crops were up we would need some way to keep the weeds in check. The tool for that would be a two-horse cultivator. If we were going to do any haying with the horses, we'd need mowers they could pull. Sam and Silver came with harnesses and collars, but we needed the pieces called eveners that connect the horses' tug chains to the tongue of a machine, and neck yokes, to hold the tongue off the ground in front. A stone boat, a sturdy sled that slides flat along the ground, for hauling a plow to the field, would be nice. A forecart would be even nicer. It's a simple, two-wheeled cart with a hitch in the back, for pulling tools or wagons. We would need a drill, for planting grain, and a potato digger. There were other things on the wish list, but this was the minimum. Our budget was slim.

The tractor had come late to this sparsely populated region, and plenty of the neighbors had used horses on their farms through the 1950s. Some of their old equipment had already gone for scrap, or been sold to antiques dealers, or plunked to rust in the front yard as decoration, encircled by impatiens in the summer, by mums and pumpkins in fall. But a good deal of it was still around, stored in the backs of barns, and we scouted those dusty corners. Sometimes, we found horse-drawn machines with their tongues lopped off, evidence of the transition time when farmers hooked old tools to their new tractors. We found other tools that had been put away whole, lovingly, all moving parts smeared with grease, and never touched for sixty years. Some we bought, other pieces were given to us. Shane Sharpe loaned us a disc harrow he'd bought but never used. An elderly woman, recently widowed, contributed her husband's old wooden grain drill, plus a hand-cranked root grinder that would make it possible to feed Delia our extra beets and carrots. Then Thomas LaFountain stopped by with an auctioneer's flyer. It didn't say so outright, but from the long list of horse-drawn tools for sale and the location of the farm, we could tell it was an Amish farm selling out. Pay dirt.

The farm was a three-hour drive southwest. We left before dawn. Yet another winter storm had been blanketing the area for a week. The farm was on a windy plateau precisely in the middle of nowhere. The snowplows had bigger roads to worry about, and the last five miles were nearly impassable, heavily drifted over with snow. We skidded and spun along, less sure of our traction than the man in the bobsled in front of us, who was driving two steady Belgian mares. There was a crate of brown hens and speckled ducks in the sled; the long hairs on the horses' chests and flanks were frosted white from their breath. We slid into the field that was serving as a parking lot, and the man driving the team whoaed his horses to ask if we would like a lift to the barnyard, his Pennsylvania Dutch vowels as flat as the wind-scoured landscape.

We'd hoped the bad weather would mean a low turnout and lots of bargains, but the Amish were undeterred. Two families were selling out, moving to a settlement in Ohio, and this was a big event. Since the Amish don't drive, I had thought it would be a local affair, but the church doesn't say you can't be a passenger, so they had come from all corners of New York and Pennsylvania in rented vans and small buses, groups of grown men who were there to buy, plus lots of teenage boys, who, I deduced, had come for the social scene. A dozen teenage girls from the local community, in spotless black skirts and shawls, their hair parted precisely down the middle, were selling coffee, sandwiches, and sugary homemade pastries in a section of the barn that had been walled off with plastic sheeting and was heated with a big woodstove. The girls were supervised by a few young married women with babies and one rather severe-looking older lady in a rigid black bonnet. A girl of about eight seemed to be the designated babysitter, dandling a well-wrapped infant on her knee while simultaneously keeping a small herd of toddlers out from underfoot and away from the stove, where a batch of doughnuts was sizzling in hot lard.

The horse equipment was parked in rows in a field outside, and Mark and I walked among it. Mark showed me what to look for—crude farm-shop welds that betray a history of breakage and repair, or badly worn joints that sometimes lurk under a bright new coat of paint. The wind was stirring up snow devils around us, and the temperature was below zero. I had heard the forecast the night before, and I'd pulled out all the stops in an attempt to stay warm: two pairs of pants, two blue goose-down parkas, one on top of the other, a pair of thick wool socks over my inadequate gloves, and a Russian Army surplus hat with furry earflaps. The bidding wasn't due to start for an hour at least, and I was already hopping up and down, trying to restore some feeling to my extremities. The Amishmen were also outside going over the machinery, but they were wearing thin black wool overcoats, and their flat straw hats didn't even cover their ears, and somehow they looked toasty. I was trying to get a close look at the hats—it seemed that some of them had bands made of black ribbon, and others had electrical tape wrapped around the crowns—when Mark pointed out that groups of the teenage boys were checking me out and chortling, apparently at my outfit, which, I admit, made me look like a giant blueberry aviator. "I think they're trying to figure out what you are," Mark said. It is something when the Amish think you dress funny.

I left Mark and headed back to the heated section of the barn, where a crowd was lining up for doughnuts. The Amish call non-Amish people English, and groups of English, neighboring farmers, their faces chapped and impassive under pushed-back caps, had begun to arrive. They were dressed almost as uniformly as the Amish, except, instead of black, they wore either plaid or camouflage. I noted a variety of abnormalities on the older people, who must have been raised at a time and in a place where birth defects and nonlethal injuries didn't merit fixing: a knurled nose like a cauliflower, a scar the size of my palm across a bald scalp, a giant mole sprouting hair on a neck that was weathered and corded with muscle, like Reni's painting of the slave of the Ripa Grande. These anomalies aside, the old people looked healthier than the young, who tended toward the obese.

The auctioneer arrived, and there was a general movement toward the other end of the barn, where the household goods and smaller farm items were stacked in lines on the floor or bunched into lots on hay wagons. The auctioneer gestured to his first item, an unremarkable set of kitchen chairs, and the crowd pressed tight for a glimpse. The household goods looked a lot like those you'd see at any rural yard sale—cheap stuff in weird colors—but the atmosphere was more like a fair, a happy sociocommercial occasion. No wonder Thomas LaFountain will drive 150 miles to go to an auction, even if he's not intending to bid on anything. "What'd you buy?" his boys will ask when he gets home. "A hamburger," he'll say.

The auctioneer began his pitch for the chairs, describing them as lovingly as if they had come directly from under his own mother's kitchen table. Shopping is a simple transaction—do I want this thing at this given price?—but an auction is relative: Do I want this thing more than the man standing next to me wants it? How much more? It's a party, a casino, a circus, or a concert, and the auctioneer is its host, its ringmaster, its conductor. The bidding began, the numbers rolling off his tongue, elided and almost incomprehensible, sandwiched between meaningless syllables and some corny one-liners. If the bidding slowed he'd look stern, taking the crowd to task for overlooking the virtues of a particular item. He had three henchmen, big, paunchy men who carried sticks and punctuated the auctioneer's song with a loud basso "HEP!" and a thump of the stick when they spotted a bid. The spotters were necessary because bidding was practically a contest in subtlety, placed with a raised eyebrow, a microscopic nod, or at most the twitch of a cheek. The spotters were on these little movements like bird dogs to the flutter of a wing. Our friends the Owenses, who are great auction goers, had warned us to watch out for the unscrupulous spotters who "HEP!" at phantom bidders to drive up the price, or for the auctioneer's shill, buried in the crowd, who guarantees bottoms on the more valuable items with house bids if they threaten to sell too low.

It was lunchtime before the household goods were sold and the bidding started on the stock, and the crowd thinned a bit as people drifted toward the woodstove for hot soup. The crate of hens went for five dollars a bird, and the ducks brought two-fifty each. The two mares we had seen drawing the bobsled were also for sale, and they were chunky, sound, and well-broke. The auctioneer pointed out that the younger one was bred to the son of a famous Belgian stallion, and due to foal in June. In effect, she was two horses for the price of one. Conventional horse wisdom says you should never buy horses at auction, but bidding was slow, and the temptation was almost too much for me. My hand twitched upward a couple times, but Mark gave me a look that said he wouldn't hesitate to hold it down physically if necessary.

The crowd returned as the auctioneer geared up to sell the machinery. He opened bidding on a horse-drawn forecart fitted with a small engine that would power the spinning shaft of any tractor-based tool, like a hay baler or a rotary tedder. The price shot up like a flushed quail, leveling out north of five thousand dollars. Who knew the plain people had such fat wallets? There were no big bargains to be had that day. Everything was in good condition, and the Amishmen knew what it was worth, and had come with cash. We fought hard and won on the two-horse cultivator, but the walking plow and the grain binder that Mark lusted after went soaring way above our budget. We comforted ourselves with the realization that the money the men were spending had been earned by farming with horses, and if they said a tool was worth good money, then there must be money to make from it. Later, a man who had noticed our bidding offered us a grain binder that he had restored. We made a deal for it and contracted for him to deliver it, along with the cultivator we'd bought, which would not fit in our car.

Before the machinery was all sold, I was rigid with cold, despite my outrageous outfit. I found myself a bench next to the woodstove in the barn where the girls were doing a brisk business in hot coffee. I must have luxuriated in there for an hour, talking to a cluster of bent old men about draft horses. Then the auction ended, and the Amishmen came streaming in. They all have the same style eyeglasses—those slightly oversize plain wire frames that the kids who took the auto shop classes in high school wore—and they have the lenses that tint dark when they're out in the sun, so when the whole lot of them walked into the warming area, it looked like a ZZ Top tribute band convention, all long beards, dark suits, and shades. Then the auctioneer came in without his microphone or his spotters and stepped up to the table stacked with leftover sweets. He picked up a bag of doughnuts and held it high over his head. "We got a sack of delicious homemade doughnuts here," he said. "Whaddaya give? Do I hear five-biddy-fie-biddy-fie?" and he launched into his well-worn song. The girls sold all their baked goods, and a bunch of Amish teenagers rode home to Pennsylvania on the crest of a sugar high.

Delia was doing her best to heal. Her scabs hung thick and heavy on the stumps of her ears, and she had a set of angry abscesses all along her neck, where we'd injected her with antibiotics in the days right after the incident. Roy took a look at them and told us not to worry, that he'd had them on his cows before, sometimes two feet long. Delia accepted them as she'd accepted everything else that had happened since she'd come to us: patiently, placidly. Her udder had healed well, though, and she was milking like crazy, three rich gallons per day.

Two people and one cow was a lopsided equation. Our refrigerator was so full of dairy products in various forms, there was no room for anything else. One morning, I opened it to find some cream, and a quart jar of milk fell on my foot. "We have to do something about this," I said. Mark had finished his breakfast and was scanning the weekly circular for useful tools. "There's a litter of piglets for sale twenty minutes north," he said. "They could drink some milk." I grabbed the phone and dialed, and before I'd hung up I'd agreed to buy four, with a fifth thrown in for free, because he had fits, the lady said, and something was wrong with his neck.

Mark was busy that morning trying to untangle the electrical panel in the west barn, so I drove by myself to pick them up. When I got there, I peered over the side of the horse stall where the piglets were sleeping in a heap and then drew back. I'd pictured creatures the size of Chihuahuas, but they were twice that size. The crate I'd brought to haul them home in was way too small. We did not own a truck, and the lady I was buying them from did not have time to haul them. I shrugged, put an old bedspread into the hatchback of my Honda, shoved the squealing pigs in, and jimmied a pallet into place in the backseat. The pigs made short work of the bedspread, which was soon crumpled uselessly in the corner, but the pallet held until the moment I pulled into the farm driveway, when they all scrambled over the backseat like invaders over a parapet. The stink of pig in the upholstery was muted until warmer weather arrived, and then it came on hard, and stayed. We fished the piglets out of the car one by one and carried them to Delia's pen, which Mark had divided down the center with scrap lumber. We named the deformed one Torque.

The pigs became my responsibility. Mark and I were getting into power struggles over every little decision that needed to be made, neither of us wanting to lose control. To diffuse tension we'd decided to split the farm in two. Each of us was captain of half of the farm. As a farm management strategy, it was awkward, but it was necessary for the preservation of our relationship at that time. When we'd divided the livestock, Mark got charge of our one-cow dairy. Lucky me, I got the pigs.

By the time they arrived, my pigs were past the coy, curly-tailed stage and well into the voracious, menacing phase. Pigs really do have terrifically gluttonous natures. They can't help it. We've bred them to be professional eaters, meat packed as fast as possible onto four stumpy legs. They can gain more than a pound a day. That kind of growth is fueled by prodigious appetite, and in a group situation, at feeding time, they are viciously competitive, using their dense bodies to check, and their sharp teeth to bite, and their deep-throated barks to intimidate. The worst part of my day quickly became the moment when I would scramble over their pen wall carrying a five-gallon bucket full of sour skim milk mixed with cornmeal and wade through a swarm of pig bodies intent on knocking me down. More than once I ended up on my back, covered in sour milk and pig manure, shoved and bitten by five frenzied beasts.

One-on-one, they were less menacing but no less troublesome. One pig had figured out how to wiggle past the wall that divided the pigpen from the cow pen, and when I arrived at the farm in the morning, I'd find her in with Delia. There was no way to get her back in the proper place without catching her, lifting her, and dropping her over the chest-high barrier. It was like catching a large greased watermelon, a shockingly fast and willful one, one with an ear-piercing squeal.

I hit pig bottom one day during the darkest week of December, when the temperature had ventured tentatively above freezing and the snow wilted into chilly, slick-bottomed puddles. I was alone on the farm, Mark off to the farmers' market in Troy, networking.

Aside from chores and milking, my only job of the day was to move the pigs out of their pen in the west barn, which they'd outgrown, and into the roomy run-in of the east barn thirty feet away, which I had already filled with a thick layer of mulch hay. I figured I could get this done quickly and then go home, stoke up the fire, and enjoy the almost unimaginable luxury of a quiet, empty house, a hot bath, and a book. The problem was that, when it came down to it, I realized I had no idea how I was going to move those pigs. They'd become too big to carry. I knew from experience that they would not herd, and if I tried to push them they would just push back. I suspected if they got loose outside they'd be gone, quite possibly for good. Okay, I thought, I'm a smart person. I can figure out how to move five pigs thirty feet. The thing to do, I decided, was to build a chute.

I filled a wheelbarrow with things I found in the machine shop that looked like they might be useful: a hammer, a saw, and—eureka!—some pieces of metal roofing, three feet wide by fifteen feet long. Then I walked back to the barns and stared at my problem. The pigpen had a door that let out onto the alley between the two barns, but the door to the run-in was all the way around on the east barn's south side. I was thinking I would somehow build a laneway for the pigs with the sheets of roofing, but I didn't have enough material to get all the way to the door of the east barn. Just then, as if on cue, a wet, sleety snow began to fall. The bath and the book that I had been looking forward to all week began to seem remote. I decided I was overthinking it, trying to come up with an elegant solution when any solution would do. We weren't building the Taj Mahal here, I reminded myself. We were trying to move five pigs thirty feet. So I picked up the saw from the wheelbarrow and began cutting a hole in the wall of the east barn run-in, directly across from the door to the pigpen.

I was struggling mightily with the sawing, making very little progress, and the sleet was dripping off the edge of the barn down the collar of my coat, when I heard a pickup idling in the driveway. I looked up to see Shep Shields, our neighbor from over the hill, hobbling toward me. Shep had become a daily visitor, bringing us small things from his barn that he thought we could use, or sometimes a box of cake he picked up at the store. On my birthday, he brought me a potted plant.

He squinted at me through the sleet. I thought about how I must look, wet, red-fingered from cold, cutting a hole in a perfectly good barn for no apparent reason. "I don't want to tell you what to do," Shep began. This, I'd found, was a very common statement in the North Country. You're not considered rude if you don't return phone calls, or if you get drunk while working, or fail to show up as promised, but telling someone how to do something is bad form and requires a disclaimer. I braced myself. "I don't want to tell you what to do," Shep said, "but that saw you're using? That's a hacksaw. You want a wood saw." And he hobbled back to his truck and left.

I was coming up against a cold, hard truth. I was well-educated, well-read, and well-traveled. I could hold my own in cocktail conversation most places in the world. But when it came to physical work, I was virtually retarded.

After I'd traded the hacksaw for a wood saw and made a pig-size hole in the barn wall, I propped the rusty roofing into a chute held together with baling twine and opened the pen door. I braced myself for a five-pig stampede, but absolutely nothing happened. I'd baited the chute and the run-in with loaves of old bread soaked in sour milk, but for once the damn pigs weren't hungry. They had no desire to leave their snug, dry pen, and no amount of shoving, shouting, begging, or cursing would make them change their minds. I was cold, wet, and exhausted, and the sun was going down. It was time to milk Delia again. I'd pinned the pigs' door open in such a way that I'd have to disassemble the entire chute in order to close it, something I was not, at that moment, willing to do. I finished the chores and left, hoping the pigs would feel bolder and hungrier in the dark, and find their way through the chute to the run-in on their own.

I fell asleep as soon as I'd stripped off my clothes and had bad dreams about pigs all night. Mark did not get home from Troy until past midnight, so I got up alone the next morning and went to the farm to milk.

It was still mostly dark when I pulled up to the barn, but as my headlights swept the alley I could see that my chute was toast. The pigs had completely flattened it, and when I got out of the car I found their little, pointy tracks all over the barnyard. I looked around. I listened intently. No sign of them. I looked in the pen and in the run-in, but both were echoey and empty. It slowly dawned on me what a bad situation this was. They could be anywhere by now, in the woods, rooting up the neighbor's semifrozen lawn, or wandering on the road, where they could cause a serious accident.

I jumped back in the car with a sick feeling and drove to the house. Mark was squirreled under the covers, deeply asleep. I told him a strategically edited version of the story, and he got out of bed and into his clothes, not happy but at least on the move. We drove to the farm in peevish silence.

The sun was fully up by then, and we could see the tracks more clearly in the melting snow. I thought about how the devil is supposed to have a cloven foot, just like the pig. Mark circled around, trying to figure out which direction they'd headed, but the tracks didn't seem to go anywhere. I was off to the barn to get a bucket of grain with which to bait them, if we ever found them, when I heard a familiar snorting bark from inside the run-in. I peered over the gate and saw one of the pigs emerging from underneath the hay, and then four other piglike lumps began to stir, hay falling from their backs. All home, all safe, exactly where I wanted them. Mark stood and watched, shaking his head. I gave him a triumphant smile, and told him I had everything under control and he could feel free to go home and back to bed. I needed to get him out of there before he noticed the hole in the side of the barn, and I needed to figure out how to fix it.

As I patched the barn with scrap lumber, pig-tight but ugly, I was forced to confront my own prejudice. I had come to the farm with the unarticulated belief that concrete things were for dumb people and abstract things were for smart people. I thought the physical world—the trades—was the place you ended up if you weren't bright or ambitious enough to handle a white-collar job. Did I really think that a person with a genius for fixing engines, or for building, or for husbanding cows, was less brilliant than a person who writes ad copy or interprets the law? Apparently I did, though it amazes me now. I ordered books from the library about construction, plumbing, and electricity, and discovered that reading them was like trying to learn in a foreign language, the simplest things—the names of unknown tools or hardware, the names for parts of structures—creating dead ends that required answers, more research. There's no better cure for snobbery than a good ass kicking.

Just before Christmas my friend Nina came to visit from California, to get a closer look at the man I was supposed to be marrying. Nina and I had been roommates our freshman year of college, put together randomly but bonded for life. She and Mark are not very different at core—both whippy-smart, loquacious, high-energy, high achievers, and also unafraid of debate, and generally certain they're right. I felt an immediate friction between them, two people who loved me but couldn't quite figure out how to like each other.

I negotiated a day away from the farm with Nina, and

we took the ferry to Burlington. Walking down the sidewalk crowded with people wearing flattering clothes, their boots not caked with manure, was disorienting, like suddenly being thrown back into civilization after an arduous trek through a jungle. We stepped into shops, and I fingered the clothes idly, unable to imagine what use they'd be to me. We looked at wedding dresses, but they were so white I didn't want to touch them, sure I still had dirt on my hands. We took a table in a café and ordered coffee. She looked hard at me in that way that means she's about to give me a talking-to. It wasn't the relationship. It was the wedding.

Nina and I have many things in common, but in some ways we're opposites. When I visited her in California, she'd planned a week's worth of adventure—spas, camping, restaurants, bookstores, wineries—made the reservations, printed out maps and an itinerary, and had them all tucked into a folder that was on the front seat of her car when she picked me up at the airport. I showed up with a duffel bag that I'd packed as the car service was waiting at the curb, wearing flip-flops because I hadn't been able to find my other shoe. Two years earlier, she and her husband, David, had thrown themselves a fabulous wedding, equal parts elegance and fun. It came off as effortless, as a good party will, but in truth it had taken a year and a half of strategic planning. Our own wedding date was set now, nine months off, and I hadn't done any of the necessary advance work. From Nina's point of view I was almost irreversibly behind schedule. She is the most loyal of friends, and she saw that it was time for an emergency intervention. She began gently, interrogatively, but built up steam.

"Have you hired a bartender yet? And what about save-the-date cards? They really should go out now. People need to make plans. And what about a caterer? Good ones book up a year in advance." She reached into her purse and pulled out a pen and began making a list. I sipped my coffee and felt my blood pressure rise. "Porta Potties," she wrote and underlined it. She paused, tapping her pen on the table. "What are you doing about chairs?" she asked. "You are going to need to rent chairs."

I had never considered chairs. When we got home and Nina had gone to bed I told Mark, with anxiety in my voice, that we were going to need to rent chairs. The conversations about the wedding, to this point, had been vague and quick, taking place over Delia's back during milking, or when we ended up in the same horse stall, mucking. There hadn't been time to sit down and plan. We both claimed to want a simple wedding, on the farm, in early October. We both wanted to avoid the craziness and tension that weddings seem to spawn. We wanted to serve great food that we grew ourselves. From there, our visions diverged. I was thinking small, maybe fifty at most. Mark was thinking somewhere around three hundred people. (On his first-draft guest list, he'd included his middle-school art teacher, a family he'd lived with for two weeks in India, and his pediatrician.) I wanted country chic, classy, maybe with a touch of irony thrown in that alluded to my urban background. Farm lite. Mark wanted *real*—he wanted to show our guests the farm *and* the manure—and he wanted cheap, not because he was cheap but because he hated waste, and because, as he accurately pointed out, we were starting a new business, and the bank account was spiraling downward at a dizzying clip.

"What's wrong with bales?" Mark said. "Why can't people sit on straw bales?" I tried to picture my mother and her friends perched on bales in their dresses, straw poking their bottoms. My mother was still spinning from my abrupt departure from the city and our express-lane courtship. She'd gotten glimpses of our lives at the farm, and they'd worried her. What she would want, next to no wedding at all, was something clean, correct, and as normal as possible considering the circumstances, with a big open bar. Not straw bales.

The fight that ensued was long and loud and ended in a draw. By the end we'd agreed only that we didn't have time for such fights, and that in the future, if one person brought up something volatile, something likely to devolve into what we were calling a time-loss argument, the other person could say "Chairs!" and the discussion would immediately be put on hold until bedtime, when we'd be too tired to fight anyway. The result was that we didn't talk about the wedding at all until it was within spitting distance of happening.

As long as I could pretend I was some kind of exchange student, destined, eventually, to return to my native land, I was fine—more than fine. I felt about the farm the same mix of emotions I'd felt about Mark when we'd met. Fascination, infatuation, exasperation, and love. But the work was so hard, and my circumstances so foreign, I could only live in the present. If I thought more than a day in advance, I'd get shaky. A trip into the outside world would leave me rattled, unsure. At Christmastime, Mark stayed on the farm to milk Delia, and I went to spend a few days with my family, with plans to return on Christmas Eve so Mark wouldn't have to spend the holiday alone. My parents had rented a house in Florida, and my brother and his wife and my sister and I met them there. It was sunny and clean and warm and comfortable in Florida, and there was a pool, and we all slept late and made easy meals from things we bought at the supermarket. We had no chores or obligations, and in the evenings we'd have cocktails and throw something on the grill and play games and talk. After a few days of this, I felt like a new person, the farm and its difficulties receding in the background. On the snowy drive home from the airport, I allowed myself to imagine a little bit of future, with Mark, on the farm, after things were organized and established and we weren't working so ridiculously hard. I glimpsed that old warm and painful idea of home. I listened to carols on the car radio and indulged in a bout of longing.

By the time I arrived at the house I'd worked myself up into a kind of seasonal-nostalgic fervor. I was determined to commit fully, and to create the home I longed for with Mark, out of whatever materials were available. We would have holiday traditions, damn it, and the traditions would start tonight. I saw us cooking a phenomenal Christmas Eve dinner together, the template for every conjugal Christmas Eve to come. I burst through the door, ready to launch into tradition making, only to find the house dark, no fire in the woodstove, nobody home. The milk pail was still in the sink, and there were dirty boots in the hallway that smelled of manure, and there was a cow halter on the dining room table. All at once this place and this life that I'd chosen felt small and dirty and squalid, and I didn't want to be there at all.

I opened the bottle of scotch I'd brought Mark as a present and poured myself a stiff drink and ate cold leftovers with my parka on, too depressed to start a fire.

Mark came home as I was about to crawl into bed. He was wearing a blanket, belted at the waist, and carrying a nasty, moth-eaten lambskin and a shepherd's crook. He'd been recruited, last minute, to play Joseph in the Nativity pageant at St. John's, and he was as lit up from his moment in the spotlight as any actor I'd ever seen in New York after a show. It was not a speaking role, he said, but he'd made the most of it, and he thought his full beard and ungroomed hair had added a touch of verisimilitude. He'd had a great time, made new friends, and he couldn't believe I was so upset just because he hadn't thought to leave me a note. We shared a drink in bed together, the clock on the church steeple striking midnight, and I cried on his chest with an emotion that I couldn't name and he couldn't understand, but through which he'd gladly hold me.

The new year began, and Delia's ears started to stink. There was a big pus-filled crack forming in the base of one of her nubbins, and when I got close to examine it, the smell of it would knock me back. Every morning I'd arrive at the farm with a bottle of warm water and some iodine, tie her to her stanchion with a halter, and swab at the stinking scab, trying to keep it open enough to drain. She would shake her head when she saw me coming, but that was the extent of her protest. The wounds were filling with granulation tissue, the raw, ugly new flesh that is the first step to healing.

The dairy where Delia had come from called to say they had another cow they could sell us, cheap, because she'd been their daughter's pet and they didn't want to ship her for beef, but they couldn't keep her because her udder was too pendulous and their laneways were very mucky, so she'd come in for milking with her teats all caked and messy with muck. She was half Jersey, and half Holstein, a heavy milker. Her name was Raye. When I was in my twenties I lived in Mexico for a year. I arrived knowing very little Spanish, and, as I was trying to learn, I would often find myself in a conversation with someone, totally lost, clinging to any familiar word that came out of their mouth, trying to piece the words together into something that made sense. When the words stopped and they looked at me like they expected a response, I invariably said, "*Sí.*" That strategy got me into some interesting situations, but it did move things along. That is the only way I can think of to explain why we bought Raye. We had too much milk already, and too little time, but we were a little lost and easily excited, and when asked a question, our default answer was "*Sí.*"

If Delia was to have a roommate, they'd need a bigger room. The west barn had a large shed built onto its west side, with a sliding door. Its framing and the exterior walls were all right, but the cheap pressboard put up on the inside was warped and crumbling. We spent a day pulling it down and packing the soft stuff into a Dumpster, and another day plucking the nails out of the now-bare studs. From the light socket we pulled a fried and desiccated bat. It must have tried to roost there, back when the electricity still worked.

Raye arrived, and she was Delia's opposite, big boned,

inky, and willful. She bellowed like a tuba. At milking time, she charged out of her stall as I hung on to her collar, about as effective as a flea. When I washed her udder, she'd wave her hoof at me, and for a week she kicked over every bucket I put under her, until I finally learned how to hold the bucket off the ground, between my knees. If Raye had been around when Delia was attacked, I decided, those dogs wouldn't have had a chance. She bossed Delia from one end of their shed to the other, but Delia was delighted to be with one of her own. When I left the barn in the evening, the last thing I'd see was Delia licking Raye shyly, her rubbery tongue making cowlicks in Raye's thick winter fur.

In January, we bought a herd of beef cattle from a farmer who was selling out. They were Scottish Highland cattle, feral-looking things, with wide horns and thick, wavy fur, some red, some black, some silver, with long bangs that hung down over their eyes. More than one person stopped to ask if we were raising yaks. We'd bought the Highlands because they were for sale nearby at a good price, and the breed came with certain advantages that fit well with our situation. They are the oldest breed of cattle on record, their genetics formed under harsh conditions. They are known for hardiness on marginal pasture, for ease of calving and good mothering, and for finishing well on grass instead of on grain. Their extremely thick coats were a benefit, too, during our hard winters. In cold spring rains, they repelled water like sheep. The downside was that they were slow growers, taking two years or more to get to slaughter weight. Also, this herd was wild. When we unloaded them, a bull calf slipped out an impossibly small gap between the trailer and the fence and took a trot all over the farm, while his perturbed mama snorted and tried to knock down a gate. He was white and fuzzy, like a big lamb. We named him Wiley.

The seeds arrived in February, a whole farm in a box. Of all the mysteries I'd encountered on the farm, this seemed the most profound. I could not imagine how several tons of food could come out of a box so small and light I could balance it on one hand. Mark and I had spent evenings poring over the seed catalogs that had arrived during the darkest week of winter, piling up next to the bed like farmer porn. I decided the glossy Johnny's catalog, with its four-color spreads of air-brushed produce, was aimed at farmers who are visually stimulated, while the scrappy Fedco catalog, just newsprint and line drawings but with gorgeous descriptions, was aimed at people like me, who got off on words. If it had been left up to me, we would have grown one of everything from the catalogs that year. In the winter squash section alone, I underlined twelve intriguing varieties, including Candy Roaster, Turk's Turban, Pink Banana, and something called Galeux d'Eysines, which the text told me meant "embroidered with pebbles." The herb sections made me completely nuts. How could you *not* order one packet each of saltwort, sneezewort, motherwort, and Saint-John's-wort, plus a sample of mad-dog skullcap, which the text said was once a folk remedy for rabies? At a buck a pop, how could you go wrong? The whole trick of seed catalogs is that they come into the house in winter, when everything still seems possible and the work of growing things is too far in front of you to be seen clearly. Luckily, Mark knew this and had quietly retrieved my list and crumpled it up, so the box that arrived at our door contained the seeds of edible things that are generally liked by humans, a reasonable number of varieties, and nothing that ended in *wort*. We sorted through the packets, separating those that would be direct-seeded in the field from those that needed to be started early, in a greenhouse, in a few short weeks. We did not have a greenhouse, but building one was on the list.

In the middle of February, Mark made a trip to Pennsylvania to collect his sugaring equipment, which he'd stored at his old farm in State College. He came back with the evaporator, a heavy iron firebox called an arch, that looked like a metal coffin, six feet by two feet, capped with a shiny stainless-steel pan. We installed it in the corner of the pavilion near the road and cut a hole in the tin roof to poke the chimney through. We borrowed a two-hundred-gallon sap tank from Thomas LaFountain, who had used it in his own sugar bush until he'd switched over from buckets to plastic tubing.

The farm was beginning to acquire form, coming together out of disparate pieces. We had the dairy cows, the beef cattle, the pigs, the hens, the seeds, and the equipment to make sugar out of trees. We had the pieces in place now, everything we needed to produce our food and the food of our as-yet-imaginary members. Everything, that is, but the hours we needed to get it all done. Raye's big udder was much harder to milk than Delia's neat little bag, and Raye also produced more milk, so no matter how early we started, the sun would be well up before the milk was put away and the milking equipment washed. And then there would be the other morning chores: the horses to be bedded and fed, the pigs to be slopped, the chickens needing to be let out of their coop, fed, watered. The beef cattle were housed in the east barn's shed, and their hay was in the west barn mow, so every day we'd throw bales to the ground and walk them over, one by one, because we didn't yet have a cart. We did not have enough hoses, so we carried a lot of water. The days were getting longer, and every moment was filled with urgent work, and the list of things to do, at the end of the day, was longer than it had been that dawn.

All the money we spent came from savings. Cash flow was a one-way stream. We ordered hundreds of dollars' worth of electric fencing, including fence chargers, step-in posts, chicken netting, and thousands of feet of the plastic electric string that we would use to make mobile pastures for the cattle and horses. We needed tools, too—not only carts and hoses but hand tools, and more machinery, and buckets and tanks and hay racks and mangers. Our account balance approached zero. Every night, we revised our to-do list, editing it down to bare essentials. I tried to let go of the desire for beautiful and to settle instead for functional, and I gained insight into why working farms look the way they do. There were three construction projects going on at any one time, and anyone who appeared at the farm was put to work. My friend Alexis came for a visit from New Orleans, where she had just finished restoring a house, and we put her to work rewiring the barns. By the time she left, we had lights. As the days lengthened, we resumed cleanup, trashing three more buildings, carting them away. We had no rhythm to our days then, no routine, and the farm was so full of emergencies—from escaped cattle to frozen pipes—that the work seeped into the hours when we ought to have been sleeping, and still we had more to do.

The tenants left the farmhouse at the end of the winter, a few months before their lease was up. We moved in and discovered it was infested with rats. The whole farm was ratty, in fact, thanks to the several tons of wheat that had been left in the granary years before and never cleared away. We did not have any furniture and were sleeping on a mattress on the floor in the downstairs apartment's bedroom, and I would wake up at night to the sound of the rats scrabbling around in the walls. We tracked the noises to the crawl space at the top of the house, and when Mark looked in there, he found innumerable nests in the insulation. If I went to the kitchen at night for a glass of water, the light would catch a sleek brown body and a long skinny tail disappearing into a hole in the wall above the stove. The phone went dead, and when we investigated, we found the rats had chewed through the line. Part of their home invasion plan seemed to include cutting us off from the outside world. After that, I worried they'd chew through the electrical wires and burn the house down with us inside. Outside, they'd gotten cozy with the pigs, eight or ten of them nosing around for scraps at one time in broad daylight. I figured we were outnumbered by a factor of a hundred.

We set traps, the kind that look like oversize mouse traps, with the springs so loaded they'd break a person's finger. We set them night after night inside the walls, where the rats had chewed holes through the wallboard, and night after night we would hear the *snap!* of a trap going off and find a dead rat in the morning. My city-raised dog, Nico, had shown no interest in hunting rats. I found a website that said if you want your dog to rat, you have to show her that rats are the enemy. So I put on rubber gloves, shucked a freshly dead rat from a trap, and took it outside. With Nico watching, I shrieked at the rat, hurled it to the ground, did violence to it with the heel of my boot, and shrieked some more. Nico watched skeptically, then tucked her tail and slunk off, thoroughly convinced that rats should be avoided at all costs. Then the rats got wise to the snap traps and we stopped catching them; the rat traffic decreased not a whit.

Another website suggested barrel traps. We sprinkled grain in the bottom of a fifty-gallon barrel and propped a two-by-four on the outside, so the rats could climb in, and another on the inside, so they could climb out. After a few days of this, we removed the inside stick, put a foot of water in the barrel, and floated grain on the water. The rats would go in but never come out. One morning we caught six this way, and we must have killed two dozen over the course of two weeks, but then they got smart to it and left the barrel alone.

Finally I went to the animal shelter and asked them for their fiercest, least adoptable inmates. I came home with three cats, two bobtailed sisters and a black-and-white. They weren't exactly the cold-blooded killing machines I'd had in mind. They were stunted, hard-luck things, not much bigger than the biggest rats. When I released them in the barn, they circled my legs and purred. When a lady came by a few days later with a box full of kittens—word had gotten around we were looking for some—I took them. I figured we'd need reinforcements.

The five kittens were just weaned, and at night they slept together in the barn, curled into a fuzzy ball. During the day they batted paper towels around the barn floor, staged elaborate ambushes and mock fights, and mewed to be picked up and petted. One morning, a week after they arrived, I flipped on the lights in the barn and there was no mewing. I found the first one, the little gray, next to the cows' stanchions, cold and stiff, and then saw two more. I picked the gray one up. Dead, it felt tinier than in life, a little rack of bones covered in soft fur. Mark came in and took it from me, examined it, parted the fur at the neck, and found a pair of vampiric puncture wounds, half an inch apart.

"It was a weasel," he said. "They suck blood."

Is the whole world just a cruel dance between eaters and the eaten? I buried the poor things in the compost pile. The two surviving kittens emerged from hiding after a few days, and we named them Mink and Marten. The weasel evaded our efforts to trap it and went on to kill a banty hen and all her chicks; then it slipped back to the underworld, through whatever steaming crack it had emerged from, never to torment us again.

But the rats began to disappear, too, little by little, first from the house and later from the barns. I never saw a cat kill one, but the cats stalked all the rats' favorite places, even took their luxurious naps in the granary, on top of the sacks of grain. Maybe the rats retreated or became less brazen. Maybe the cats were eating the rat babies. Whatever it was, we were gaining on them.

Part Three
Spring

It was a strange betrothal. Romantic, but different from what that word had meant to me in my old life, when it had been almost synonymous with intrigue. Mark didn't even know how to have a relationship like that. When he was in third grade, he wrote long, involved love notes to a series of girls in his class. The boys would tackle him on the playground, steal the notes from his pockets, and read them out loud from the top of the monkey bars. That didn't stop him from writing them. His biggest crush that year was on a girl named Claudia. He used his allowance to buy her a glittery poster—white unicorn in the foreground, castle and rainbow in the background—and when she told him primly that she couldn't accept it, he tried to give it to another girl. She rejected it, too, so he shrugged, took it home, and hung it on his own wall. He was undaunted then, and remained so. It would never occur to him to be coy. He had no hidden agenda, was plotting no reversal. He had shown me who he was the first time we met, and had never been cagey about his intentions.

So the romance between us came from some new and different source, from being yoked together with a common goal, a tight little team of two. I imagined this was what it would feel like to forge a relationship at boot camp or be marooned together, albeit on a very fertile island. We woke up and fell asleep talking about stock, seeds, drainage, tools, or how to eke another minute out of the day by streamlining a chore, saving steps. Our bodies were so tired. Sometimes, in the brief moment between bed and sleep, we'd touch our fingertips together, an act we cynically called farmer love. If we were destined to have children, I remember thinking, they'd have to be conceived in the dead of winter, when nights were long.

I had never in my life been so dirty. The work was always dirty, beyond what I'd previously defined as dirty, and it took too much energy to keep oneself out of it. I had daily intimacy not just with *dirt* dirt but with blood, manure, milk, pus, my own sweat and the sweat of other creatures, with the grease of engines and the grease of animals, with innards, with all the stages of decomposition. Slowly, the boundary of what I found disgusting pushed outward. The thought of bathing was unappealing at the end of the chilly spring day, with the unheated bathroom so far from the woodstove and morning milking so near. Some nights I would only peel off my outer layer of clothes before leaping under the thick comforter, leaving the pieces at the foot of the bed for easy access in the morning dark. My wardrobe from the city had sifted down to one small drawer of unruined things, reserved for off-farm use, which meant they never got worn. The rest had been added, piece by piece, to the general-use bin. I discovered the insulating properties of silk, which gave my collection of lingerie new purpose. Some days I farmed in a black cashmere V-neck that I used to call my first-date sweater. In its youth I'd pampered it with dry cleaning and padded hangers. Now it was flecked with hay, two holes worn in the elbows.

I let my hair grow out, not by conscious choice but because making and keeping an appointment to cut it never reached the top of the priority list. I forgot to pluck my eyebrows. I hardly ever looked in the mirror, and when I did I saw that all the outdoor work was etching new lines around my eyes, weathering my complexion, bringing out the red tones, the freckles. I began to feel the weight of my skin on my brow, my cheeks folding down at the sides of my mouth. My new life was marking me. It was happening so quickly. There were intermittent spells of resistance, during which I'd pluck and moisturize and exfoliate, and then there was a period of grieving for my old self, who seemed to be disappearing toward the horizon, and then I relaxed into it.

March was a tense and slightly dangerous time, like a border crossing between two conflicting countries. It's not the deprivations of winter that get you, or the damp of spring, but the no-man's-land between. The weather was beyond unpredictable, zero some nights, forty others, with winds that tore loose the tin on the barn roofs and made the horses wild in their pasture. In the fields, the snow took on a dull, depressed look, ceding more and more territory each day to the mud. Beside the driveway, the spiky piles of scrap metal came unglued from the thawing ground. On warm days, the mud in front of the barn was deep enough to grab and hold our boots. The potholes became a menace. Melting snow revealed two small out-buildings, undone by the weight of winter, resting under folded roofs. We skulked around, cold feet in wet boots.

Out in the pasture, the Highland cattle had mites; they scratched themselves with their horns or against the trees and shed out in clumps, pink skin showing through in patches. Then came the dysentery. It started with the biggest steer, a white fellow with one long horn. Every few minutes he'd lift his tail and send an alarming jet of watery, brown liquid streaming out behind. Two days later the brown liquid was tinted deep red and there were cords of mucus and sloughed-off intestinal lining in it, and the steer's condition deteriorated, his coat going dull, midribs showing. We consulted the Owenses, who said there wasn't much to do for it but watch for the turn-around, which happened five days later. The steer picked up as quickly as he went down, first recovering a little light in his eyes, then nibbling at the rougher bits of hay, the faucet of his intestines slowing from a stream to a trickle. Another of the Highlands had it by then, and we thought shelter might do the herd some good, so we moved them to the east barn run-in. The first day we watched them jostle one another for hay. The next morning, one of the yearling steers was standing alone, roach-backed and shivering. He looked like he'd been shot in the ribs with a large-caliber bullet. He'd been gored.

We called the Owenses, and Neal and his brother, Donald, came over to have a look. The steer's fate depended, they said, on whether or not the horn had pierced an intestine. If not, he would probably heal, but if so, there would be no hope. Donald and Mark shouldered him into a wall, the steer still strong enough to give the two big men a good challenge, and Donald drew some fluid from the wound with a syringe and smelled it. There was the telltale stink of manure, the sign of a leaking intestine. There was nothing to do but slaughter the yearling right away. Once he was skinned and hanging, we could see the patch of infected meat around the wound, stained chartreuse, so bright and vivid it was almost neon. We cut it out and cut out some meat around it for good measure and threw it on the ground. Nico snapped it up and slunk away, and she looked pleased for days. The rest of the meat we butchered into packages for our freezer.

The cold, wet weather wasn't kind to the other animals, either. The horses sank to their fetlocks in the mud, and they didn't move far from their hay. The pigs had it the worst. We'd moved them out of the barn to pasture, and Mark had made them a shelter from a round fiberglass irrigation tank that he'd cut in half and dubbed the pigloo. We filled it with several bales of straw, and when the pigs were all cuddled up inside it was cozy, steam rising out of the chimneylike hole in the top. Outside the pigloo, though, the pasture was saturated, and the pigs had churned it to deep mud. Soon they were reduced to a turtlelike lumber, their sharp trotters sinking almost to the hilt. We fenced in a higher, adjacent section of pasture, and they came onto firm ground tentatively, like sea-legged sailors just off ship. A brown gilt with black spots hung back. She was too well-trained to the boundary of her old pasture and would not transgress it, even when the electric string was removed. She paced and grunted nervously, while the other pigs rooted for last year's grass. We were late for milking, so we left her there by herself. It was two whole days before her loneliness trumped her fear and she crossed.

Funny that out of this scabby and difficult season flows all the sweetness of the North Country year. We got another storm, a foot of heavy snow, and then the clouds cleared and the night froze hard. The next day the sun rose with new energy. Mark and I were eating our lunch at noon and heard a thick sheet of ice tear free from the roof of the farmhouse, followed by the drip and patter of melt from the eaves. With that, the mood of our whole world changed. We'd crossed the border into friendlier territory. The sap was rising in the trees.

The sap buckets were scrubbed and the spiles were ready and waiting. We'd planned to lash Thomas's sap tank to a small wagon, to be pulled through the woods by the horses. Everything was in order, except that the snow in the woods was too deep for wheels. We needed a sled—a jumper, the Owenses called it—and we needed it soon. When Neal and Donald Owens's father was young, the family farm ran on horsepower, and everyone sugared. If anyone knew how to make a jumper, it would be Mr. Owens.

Mr. Owens arrived with Neal, in his seventies and sparely built. He looked as though he'd been weathered down from Neal's bulk to their common essential form, which was hard and locustlike, with a knobby nose and penetrating eyes the blue of a Spode teacup. Unlike the other older farmers we'd met, who favored feed-company caps and T-shirts, Mr. Owens was sharply dressed, in a cowboy hat and pointy boots with high slanted heels and a smart Western-style shirt. The wallet in the back pocket of his jeans was joined to his belt loop with a chain, trucker-style. Mark and Neal and I walked him through the machine shop and the east barn, giving him the tour, and he took in the details in perfect silence. He grew up on a farm within three miles of us, and he'd certainly seen our place a million times in his life and knew its corners better than we did. Then we all walked to the west barn, where Sam and Silver were in their stalls, picking at a flake of hay. I could see Mr. Owens perk up then, and he broke off from our group, where Mark and Neal were debating how many bales would fit in the loft. Mr. Owens fingered the harness hanging on a hook and then went to the horses. He stepped into the stall, murmuring "whoa" in a low voice, and ran a hand along Silver's shoulder, down both front legs, stepped back to get a good look at how the horse was put together. He gave a little nod.

"This how he hooks 'em?" he asked, pointing to Sam, the taller horse, on the left side of the stall, and Silver, shorter but stockier, on the right. I nodded. "Why, that's Canadian style!" he hooted. "We always hooked our bigger horse on the nigh side." One hand on Silver's flank, he told me he'd gotten his own first team of horses when he was a boy of ten or eleven. His father's horses were full-size drafts, but his first team was a pair of Percheron-Morgan crosses, a gelding and a mare, small horses with good feet and big hearts and brains. "That's the Morgan in them, you see," he said. They could work a whole hot summer day at haying alongside his father's big team without giving up. His first job as a boy was to use his team to lift loads of loose hay from the wagons into the mow, using a grapple hook. The grapple was on a pulley and track that ran back into the mow. That little team of his was so smart he could wrap the lines around the rail and send them along on their own. They knew where to stop, and Mr. Owens, who was known then as young Donald, would release the grapple load of hay to its proper place in the mow, and the horses would turn around and come back to the place where they started, ready to begin again. While he was telling me this story, his face had come to life, as though he were talking about a lost first love. Then he lapsed back into silence and his face went still.

We walked to the woods west of the barn, Neal breaking a trail in front, Mark next, lugging the chain saw, and Mr. Owens following, spry and silent, a knitted cap on now in place of the cowboy hat. We were looking for hardhack, the local name for hop hornbeam, a heavy, dense hardwood that wears extremely well and is, according to Mr. Owens, the very best material from which to make a jumper. Halfway up the hill to the sugar bush, he raised an oracular hand and pointed out a pair of twelve-foot saplings, bowed slightly at the thin end, as though they were aspiring all along to be runners.

I ran to the barn to get Silver, while Mark went to work with the chain saw. By the time I got back up the hill he had three saplings—the two hardhack runners plus a straight young ash, destined to be our tongue—felled and limbed. We wrapped a logging chain around them and hitched it to Silver, who pulled the three trees home through the snow with about as much effort as it would take me to haul home a trio of toothpicks.

In the machine shop, we bound the hardhack runners to

wooden braces and decked them over with pine boards to make a sturdy platform, six feet by eight. Nobody had built a jumper in our neighborhood for years, and when word got around, our neighbors came to see, some bringing their woodworking tools, some just standing at the margins, watching. The jumper took on form, low to the ground, rough but elegant, its lines as natural as the trees it was made from. Mr. Owens directed, pointing out where to add more bracing, how to tie in the runners so they'd stay straight and true. As we were getting ready to attach the tongue, a disagreement arose over some detail that Mr. Owens insisted on and the others—his sons and Mark and a whole shop full of younger men now—deemed illogical. Mr. Owens got quietly peeved and went and sat in the truck for the rest of the day, so he missed the inauguration of the jumper, which was too bad. I stepped Sam over the new ash tongue, and Mark hooked the four tug chains to the evener, and I sat down on the green-smelling planks with the lines in my hands, and the horses leaned into the collars. The first few yards in the driveway were hard going, peeling the bark from the bottoms of the runners, and then we hit the snow and were free.

I'd spent a lot of hours with the horses by then, not all of them easy. Harnessing was still too much for me. I'd struggle to lift the seventy-pound tangle of leather and hames up onto the horses' backs day after day, and every day I'd be defeated. I could thread my arm under the britchen and saddle and grasp the hames down low, one in each hand, like I'd seen Jimmy

Cooper do it, and I could carry it to the horses, and I could even lift the far hame up high over my head and nudge it inch by inch over the withers. But then the rest of the harness would press awkwardly into my neck, cutting off the blood to my brain, and I'd go faint and have to start all over again, my arms more exhausted with each try. I hated asking Mark to help me. With his strength, and from his height, he could pick up the harness and place it on a horse's back as easily as if it were made of twine. I would spend a half hour damaging my brain cells and exhausting myself before going to find Mark, who kept insisting it was just a matter of technique.

The trouble did not end once the harness was on. I was getting hammered, again, by my own hubris. I had ridden horses all my life, spent most of my adolescence talking or reading or thinking about them. I assumed all those skills and all that knowledge could be seamlessly transferred, that I would just switch from being a rider to being a teamster, from up on top to down behind. The way I looked at it, Mark had the farming experience and I had the horse experience, so we were a package, and there was no reason we couldn't jump right in and do it, zero to sixty the first season. As we plotted out our vegetable fields at the end of that first winter, we planned forty-inch spacing between our rows—an incidental detail, except that, once we'd committed to it, we would be forcing ourselves to rely only on horsepower for the whole season, since the tractor wheels would not fit between rows with such a spacing.

When Mark asked me if I thought we could do it, I said yes, but I felt a shiver of misgiving. Already I'd had some minor mishaps. I'd forgotten to attach a line to the outside of Sam's bit once, traveled like that all the way through the barnyard, and discovered it only when I couldn't get him to turn to step over the tongue of the wagon. Another time, I'd backed the harnessed horses out of their stalls, and, while I was pulling on my gloves to drive them out of the barn, I watched helplessly as Silver swung his big butt around until he was nose-to-nose with a freaked-out Sam, who began backing toward me. In this configuration, my lines were useless, and it was only luck that got me to the horses' heads in time, to bring them back into alignment before they'd torn up their mouths or entangled themselves in lines and scared themselves silly. We added a chain, after that, that hooked the horses' rear ends together loosely at the hip, a safety measure we should have been using from the beginning.

Once they were hitched, I found the team more excitable than they'd been when I'd driven them at Gary's. On cold mornings, Sam would pull so hard at his bit that my arms were exhausted, and, when we stopped to load something into a wagon, I had a hard time getting them to calm down and stand still. At the time I blamed it on adjustment to their new home, but now I know it was only my own inexperience, and a series of mistakes that I made—some big, stupid ones, but mostly subtle errors in judgment—that made the horses lose trust in me, a little bit each time we went out. They began to suspect that I was not fit to be in charge, and, frankly, so did I. What I should have done then was stop trying to do work with them and apprentice myself to an experienced teamster for a year or two, but at the time, that seemed out of the question. We were out of money, and we were committed to growing food for the season that was just around the corner. And so I faked it, and hoped for the best.

I had been hitching every day since the horses arrived, to move wood or loads of hay, to haul manure, any job I could think of to gain experience before the growing season started. I studied the way the horses moved, their likes and dislikes, their working personalities. Sam was the overachiever, up on the bit, head high, always trying to stay a few inches ahead of Silver. I hitched Sam to a wagon to haul our trash to the dump, and as soon as we hit the road he picked up his feet and arched his neck, as though he were in a parade. I think the image he held of himself was light and quick and proud—an Arabian, or a Thoroughbred, anything but a narrow-chested, old workhorse. But he was dutiful and willing, no matter how humble the work. Silver was the burly one, Sam's opposite. He was thickly muscled, with the neck of a steroid-addled linebacker, and he was a bit of a laggard. If I was not careful to hold Sam back and urge Silver on, Silver would drop farther and farther behind until his side of the evener rested against the cart, leaving his tug chains slack, letting Sam pull the whole load. His favorite pace was a doleful walk, but he could pull the weight of the world when he wanted to. The first time I saw him do it, we'd hitched to an old wagon to bring a load of split firewood out of the woods. It was wet, and the loaded wagon got bogged down in a patch of half-frozen mud, sinking almost to the axles. I'd been driving the team only a few weeks, and I didn't know yet how much they could pull. This, I was about to learn, was

Silver's area of expertise, the kind of work he was made for. He flicked an ear back, listening, and when I asked them to pull I saw Silver gather those gorgeous muscles of his and throw his formidable shoulders into the collar, focused, digging in, pushing off until the wagon rocked clear of the mud. We did not have to unstack that load, or any other as long as Silver was with us.

The day after the jumper was finished the weather turned too cold for sugaring. There was fresh snow on the ground, and it was clear and sunny, and the horses were feeling particularly spry. They fidgeted while Mark and I hitched them to a splintery wagon we'd pulled out of the weeds and rehabilitated, and when we set off down the farm road they picked up their feet and tossed their heads. We were traveling to the middle of the farm to pick up a load of mulch hay from where it had been stacked for several years, under the roof of a large metal barn. I sat on the deck of the wagon, and it whizzed along in its track, around the west barn, to a flat, high place that overlooked the field we'd named Long Pasture. The road turned down a hill and ran along a low, frozen swamp stamped with deer tracks, and then into a fifty-acre field.

The barn that held the hay was open on both ends, and its metal sides were coming loose, flapping in a gusty wind. I drove the team inside and stayed on the wagon, holding the lines, while Mark hefted the bales onto the deck and stacked them. The noise of the flapping metal made the horses antsy, and I wasn't paying attention to Mark's stack until it was already five tiers high. I wasn't sure they could pull that much weight up the big hill on the way home. "Only one way to find out!" Mark said as he started another tier. In most of my relationships, I'd considered myself the risk taker, the one who wanted to do more, stay out later, order another round. It occurred to me that the man I was supposed to be marrying was accustomed to finding his edge by falling off of it, catching it by a fingernail, and clawing his way back up.

It was a mile back to the barns, and Mark rode on top of the stack, twelve feet off the ground. I was driving the horses from the front of the wagon, where he'd built me a little nook out of bales. The stack towered behind me. On the flat, frozen ground, Sam and Silver handled the load easily, but when we reached the hill, they quickened their pace. They wanted to take it at a trot, to build up momentum and make the pull a little easier. The ground was slippery and I should have insisted on the walk, but I didn't know any better, so I let them trot, and they picked up steam. Halfway up the hill we hit a pothole, and I felt the stack yaw behind me, and I heard a hoot from Mark, way up over my head. I looked behind me and saw the stack careening from side to side. In glancing backward I'd taken my attention away from the horses, and they'd grabbed the opportunity to increase the pace, Sam at a tight little canter now, and Silver trotting like a maniac. One more bump on the path and the whole stack of bales went over, Mark with it. I whoaed the horses, who couldn't figure out why they'd been so suddenly relieved of their load. Silver swung his head around and stared, and Sam stood, ears pinned, looking anxious, and it was very quiet. I was not sure if Mark was under the hay or in the ditch, dead or gravely injured, and then I heard him laughing from the other side of the pile, and he popped up, covered in snow, and Silver bobbed his head as though he were in on the joke.

Sugar bush. Even the words are pretty and sweet. From up on the hill, through the bare trees, I could see each field and pasture framed by its hedgerow, all the way to the lake a mile away. The farmhouse was the warm color of Jersey cream against the blue-white snow, all its rough edges smoothed, like an aging beauty flattered by candlelight. Inside the sugar bush the snow muted the rustle of beech leaves and the clink of the harnesses and our voices, and standing still with the horses I felt like an interloper in nature's bedroom.

The sun was warm, but the snow was deep and heavy, and the horses labored to break a trail, their weight shifted to their back ends, forelegs reaching high. They still had their winter coats, and they were soon soaked with sweat. When we broke through drifts the snow came up and over the front of the jumper to where I sat, like waves over the prow of a ship. The jumper was stacked with buckets and their tops, and a box of thin metal spiles.

Making a sugar bush is a process of elimination. Over years and generations the ash and pine and birch are logged out, leaving a monopoly on sunlight and nutrients for the sugar maples. Unrestricted, the trunks of the old trees grow so big you can't wrap your arms halfway around them, and the tops spread and unfold into the open, elegant, vaselike shapes that children draw when they draw trees in kindergarten. The Springs, who had owned the farm until the 1980s, were the last family to use these woods, and they'd made a good road that cut the sugar bush in half, north to south, and another that ran uphill, east to west, forming a long-armed cross. There was a rougher road that curved between the arms of the cross, through the southeast quadrant, where the population of maples was thickest and the slope steepest. Five years earlier, the sugar bush had been ravaged by a monumental ice storm that had crippled the North Country for a week. Some of the maples had been snapped off at the top or stripped of their biggest limbs. Mark and I had spent a few afternoons clearing logs from the roads, nipping back errant branches so the horses could pass without getting whipped in the eye. Mark was so geeky about trees that when he was young he collected leaves and twigs, labeled them, and put them in photo albums. He had tagged the maples with bright pink ribbon, pointing out their opposite branching, each limb and branch and twig mirrored by a twin, a trait shared, he said, only by ash and dogwood; the bark of the younger sugar maples was the smooth gray of elephant skin, thickened into overlapping scales on the older ones.

Mark struggled from tree to tree through drifts to his knees. He drilled a five-sixteenths-inch hole into the tree, angled up just slightly, so that the sap would drip out. Then he hammered a small metal spile into the hole, which was already wet with sap. He hung a bucket on the spile and topped it with a little tin roof. We made our way along the main road like that, Mark running up and down the hill to the jumper for more buckets and spiles while the horses and I struggled to break a trail. The loop of rough road in the sugar bush's southeast corner was deeply drifted, and we decided not to chance it.

By the time half the trees were tapped, steam was rising from the horses' backs, and they were blowing hard. Silver's mood turned petulant, no matter that the humans were working at least as hard as he was. By afternoon we were finished, with 170 buckets hung, but Silver had gone on strike—ears pinned flat against his big bullet head, one back hoof flashing back to kick at the tug chains—and had to be coaxed even to pull the jumper *downhill,* toward home.

Maple sap is mostly water, with a sugar content that averages around 4 percent. It takes about forty gallons of sap to make one gallon of syrup, and all that water must be driven off drop by drop in the form of steam. Between here and there was a lot of firewood. Mark and I put the horses up in their stalls, blankets over their wet backs, and attacked the woodpile, smashing log after log of seasoned ash into kindling-like pieces until the pile toppled over on itself and we dragged ourselves to bed, worn-out. The weather radio was the last sound I heard, predicting a hard-frozen night followed by a warm, sunny day. The next morning we ran up the hill to check the nearest open-crown tree and found it running hard, not with the expected drip-drip-drip but with an actual trickle.

By afternoon the buckets on the best trees were three-quarters full, and we strapped the sap tank to the jumper and set out for the sugar bush. Silver was rested and full of corn, resigned to the work now, sensing purpose. Up on the hill, Mark followed yesterday's tracks from tree to tree and came waddling back, a full five-gallon bucket in each hand. He tipped the buckets into the tank on the jumper, which was fitted with a filter. Later in the season, when the weather stayed warm, the sap in the buckets would be a dirty yellow, full of dead bugs and moths, drawn to its fatal sweetness. But the first run was clear and clean as springwater. Mark stopped to hold a big bucket to his mouth and drink awkwardly, the sap running down his cheeks and under his sweater and around the back of his neck. I handed him the lines and jumped off my place on the sled and plunged my mouth directly into a full bucket. Whole poems could be written about the taste of the first run's sap, icy and sweet and redolent of wood.

Three hours later, we came back down the hill with a full tank of sap. We bucketed it into a 250-gallon stainless-steel holding tank that we'd scavenged from a defunct dairy and hung from the rafters of the pavilion with chain.

There's nothing complicated about making syrup from sap. All you have to do is keep boiling. The sap becomes more and more concentrated until the sugar content reaches 66 percent, and that's syrup. Anyone with a pan and a fire can do it. But to make things go faster, and to handle 250 gallons at once, you do need some special equipment.

The evaporator has two main parts: the arch, where the fire goes, and the pan, which sits on top and holds the boiling sap. Our arch is six feet long and two feet wide. The pan is made of stainless steel and has a fluted bottom, to increase the surface area that's in contact with the fire and speed up evaporation. It is fitted with a series of floats and valves, so that cool sap is constantly flowing into the pan to replace the water that is driven off as steam. The inside of the pan is baffled so that the boiling sap flows from the back of the pan to the front, growing thicker and more concentrated as it comes. When it reaches the front of the pan, it can be let into a separate section called the finishing pan, where it is closely monitored. When the thermometer in the finishing pan reads seven degrees higher than the boiling temperature of water, you have syrup. You can double-check with a hydrometer, which measures its density. There is not much room for error. If your syrup is too thin, it will sour. If you let it get too thick, it will crystallize in its jars. After you draw off the finished syrup, you pour it through a thick feltlike filter, to remove the gritty mineral substance called sugar sand, which tastes terrible and clouds the syrup.

It was a perfect week for sugaring. Every night, the temperature dipped down well below freezing, and the days warmed into the thirties. We harnessed the horses at noon and made the rounds. By the end of the week the snow was almost gone, and we moved the tank from the jumper to a wagon.

I liked running the evaporator. Mark was busy nailing together wooden flats to start our seeds, so it was quiet, solitary work that started two hours before dawn. I had never been a morning person in the city, but on the farm I'd learned to love being outdoors before light. I felt like I was sharing some kind of secret with the unhuman things around me, the birds not yet stirring in the trees, the mud quiet on the ground. I carried provisions to keep up my strength: a French press of ground espresso beans, to be brewed not with water but with boiling sap for an electrifying drink that had to be sipped in small quantities; also, a dozen eggs and a shaker of salt. Thomas LaFountain had taught me to drop the eggs one by one into the finishing pan, where they would crack with heat and the thickening sap would seep into the cracks and darken and sweeten the hard-boiled eggs, which are fished out with a long spoon and peeled and eaten hot with a heavy sprinkling of salt. I took a plate of pickles, too, an antidote in case I accidentally overdosed on sweet.

Humming, I adjusted the valves on the evaporator and cleared the ashes from the firebox. I arranged balls of newspaper and the day's first pieces of kindling, and I had turned to find a match when suddenly a bird rushed out of the firebox, flying so close to my face I felt the air from its wingbeats against my cheek. I saw a flash of black wing and heard one alarmed chirp and it was gone. "Lucky bird!" I yelled after it and put a match to the paper.

The heat builds fast, and in two or three minutes steam was rising from the pan full of sap, a sweet mist. In another few minutes, the surface began to convulse, and the steam was a solid column, too much for the hole in the roof. The steam spilled along the rafters, filling the space under the roof, creating thick clouds that condensed on the beams and by sunup began to drip on my head.

At last, I'd found something on the farm that I was a natural at. In the house, Mark was always complaining that I made too much fire. He did have a point. I had burned holes in the woodstove's thick steel interior, and I once made a room so hot that a candle on the shelf near the stove wilted. Mark is never cold, and he would fret over my profligate use of firewood and sit pointedly as far from the stove as possible, stripped down to a T-shirt. If I was comfortable, he was sweating. As a matter of compromise, I'd learned some restraint in the house, but the whole point of the evaporator is to run it the way I like it, like a freaking inferno. I stoked it every few minutes with thin, long pieces of wood that burned like chopsticks. The fronts of my thighs were soon stinging and pink.

I fell into an absorbing rhythm. Stoke the fire. Skim any dirty foam from the top of the pan. When it gets too foamy, like a pot of oatmeal about to boil over, add a sliver of lard and the foam disappears. Check the level of sap in the pan. Check the thermometer in the finishing pan. Stoke. Skim. Once you have a fire going you can't leave the evaporator, even for a moment. If you run out of sap or a valve gets stuck and the pan boils dry, the flames will eat through the thin metal and destroy your expensive equipment. I've never seen this happen, but I have been warned. Just before noon the level of sap in the storage tank was getting low. I stopped stoking the fire and let it die down. Four gallons of new syrup were safe in quart jars, not a bad morning's work.

In early April the maples budded, turning the sugar bush a hazy red. The sap becomes acrid after budding, so that was the end of sugar season. We'd made fifty gallons of syrup for the members, enough for all of us to enjoy a truly local source of sweetness. Instead of wishing for cold nights, we began looking forward to warmth, to greens. In the cellar of the farmhouse, the selection of roots Rob gave us at the beginning of winter had thinned to a few rubbery carrots, potatoes, and onions, and there were still weeks to go before the ground would be warm enough to send forth the first tonic greens. For dinner I searched the kitchen, found nothing of interest except a piece of bacon that we'd smoked last time we'd slaughtered a pig. No bread in the house, only a half bag of store-bought rice. "Slim pickings," I told Mark. "Not even you could make a decent meal of this." He walked outside with the shotgun and I heard a single blast, and then he came back up the driveway with four limp pigeons.

I held one, still warm and supple. I guess the ubiquity of the pigeon in the city had made me blind to its beauty. If they were rare, I realized, we'd paint their portraits and praise their coloring, the slate feathers with a lavender cast, the flash of rainbow at the neck. When I was a city person you couldn't have paid me to touch a pigeon, let alone eat one, but with my newfound understanding of the work it takes to raise animals for meat, I was grateful that, in this case, nature had done the raising for us. Moreover, I knew what these pigeons had been eating, and it wasn't garbage or the stale crumbs out of some creepy old lady's scrap bag. I'd watched them stuff themselves all winter on the very expensive organic corn and wheat we were feeding the pigs and chickens. They were almost too fat to fly, and the flock had grown so big they blotted out whole sections of the barn roof when they landed. They nested in the cupola of the east barn, safe from the cats, who watched from below with twitchy tails.

Mark showed me how to pluck the feathers from the breast, pin the tail feathers under one foot, stick two fingers through the skin under the breastbone, and pull. The breast came away from the body with a little sucking sound, exposing the entrails. We picked out the hearts and livers and put them in a bowl. Mark cleaned the feathers from the legs and then cut them from the bodies, which we skinned so we wouldn't have to pluck them. Heads, entrails, and wings went to the cats, who were circling eagerly.

Inside, we boned and rinsed the meaty breasts. There were eight pieces, each one the size of a walnut and dark red. I put a pot of rice on to boil and plucked some stray feathers from the legs, and cut off the feet. The legs, the tiny hearts, the backs, the livers, a slice of onion, half a carrot, and a sprig of dry thyme were covered with water and set on the stove to simmer into stock. I caramelized a large skillet of sliced onion while Mark wrapped each breast in a paper-thin piece of bacon. The breasts went under the broiler, the bacon melting into them as they cooked. I made a dark roux, loosened it with pigeon stock, added the chopped giblets, salt and pepper, a palmful of dried sage, a few crushed juniper berries gleaned from the trees behind the barn, and a splash each of bourbon and maple syrup. The meal came together like a great thrift-store outfit: elegant and outré all at the same time. Mark heaped our plates with rice, then a layer of caramelized onion, then four breasts each, and a generous spoonful of the sauce, which was dark brown and glossy. The breasts were about as far from chicken as you can get and still be eating fowl: densely textured, the color of beef, and full of wild game flavor. The effect, on the whole, was a plate to celebrate the end of sugaring, paired to the season like other people pair their courses to wine. The sweet dash of syrup and the smoky bacon evoked the wood-fired evaporator, and the bourbon celebrated the passing of winter, the arrival of spring.

*   *   *

A farm is a manipulative creature. There is no such thing as finished. Work comes in a stream and has no end. There are only the things that must be done now and things that can be done later. The threat the farm has got on you, the one that keeps you running from can until can't, is this: do it now, or some living thing will wilt or suffer or die. It's blackmail, really.

We scrambled for a week to catch up with work we'd put off during sugaring. When the weekend came, we still had to slaughter a steer. We were at the very edge of burning out and had decided that, after the steer was slaughtered and hung, we'd take half a day off, catch the ferry to Vermont, and have lunch. I let myself imagine sitting down and being served by someone else, a voluptuous thought. If we were finished by eleven, we could be back in time for evening milking.

Mark and I drove the beef herd up from pasture as soon as it was light enough to see, into a temporary paddock we'd built with electric fence. Our bull snuffed along its perimeter, sniffed the air, trumpeted. He was a massive brindled Highland named Rupert, with sleepy eyes and horns as thick as small trees at the base. It was raining steadily, and it had been raining all night. As the herd of thirty milled, our slapped-up paddock quickly turned to mud. Mark had gone to the house to get the gun, and I stood watch in my dripping rain gear and boots. One of the cows, a twitchy, reactive individual named Parker, was coming into heat. She was half Highland, half Dutch Belted. Somehow, she'd gotten a load of neurotic genes from both sides of her pedigree, and she could jump like a horse.

When we moved the herd, the rest of the cattle would amble along calmly, while Parker would buck and kick and run full speed, sometimes going headlong into the fence. One morning shortly after she'd arrived, she was missing half her tail, a fine spray of blood still coming from the stump when she twitched it over her back. I found the brushy end of it in the grass. The only theory we could come up with was that one of her neighbors had stepped on it while she was sleeping, and, feeling herself caught, she'd panicked. So it was this neurotic cow with a stub-ended half tail who was coming into heat in our flimsy, muddy paddock, and that was not good. Rupert nosed her from behind, his lip curled back in the half-pornographic, half-comical flehmen response, pushing cows and calves out of his way. Parker was not yet at the phase called standing heat, when she would happily accept the bull's advances. Instead, she darted from one end of the paddock to the other, moaning, trailing pheromones behind her. The look in her eye was even nuttier than usual, a lurid glow.

I decided to go to the barn for a load of hay, hoping a snack would calm everyone down. Halfway there, I heard a cracking sound followed by a chorus of bawling. The corner post—a two-by-two stake of oak—had snapped, and a section of electric fence lay popping and sparking on the wet ground. Parker was at the gap, Rupert behind her. She considered the situation for a moment, and then, because she was Parker, she jumped. Rupert followed, lifting his heavy body through the air on stumpy legs, and two older cows and their calves came next, pulled through behind Rupert by their herd instinct. One of the calves snagged the popping fence with a hind leg, and the plastic line stretched taut and snapped, so even that minor barrier was gone, and the herd flowed freely into unconfined space. For a few seconds, they did not know what to do with their freedom, and I thought I might be able to haze them back through the gap into the sagging paddock and hold them there until Mark returned, but they regained their volition, became a river of hair and horns, and flowed down the driveway toward the road.

We almost had them at the house. Mark came out with the gun as they were thundering toward him. They eyed him and banked right, onto the front lawn. Now they were loosely boxed on three sides by a sturdy pasture fence, the house, and a stream. The pasture fence had a gate in it, and it was open, so all we had to do was funnel them toward it. We were both thinking of a story that had circulated that spring, of a herd that had gotten loose in Westport, the lakeside town to our south. Those cattle were loose for days, wreaking havoc on yards and flower gardens, getting steadily more freaked out and less manageable, until the owner finally called in a hunter, who gunned them down. It was a total loss, the cattle so tattered, all they could do was bury them. They were Highland cattle, too.

So we pressed gently, trying to cover the escape route around the side of the house, letting the leaders get a look at the good grass in the pasture. They mooed and milled, unsure, and then good old, amiable Rupert stepped through the gate, followed by Parker and a few cows and their calves. Then the whole herd pressed toward the gate, and Mark and I smiled at each other over their backs. The cattle were calmly fanning out on the pasture and we were almost there when Parker lit the fuse of anarchy. She bucked and kicked her way along the fence, stirring up the others. She was soon followed by a group of galloping cows. If the situation weren't so serious, it would have been comical. They looked like a group of thick-middled matrons on a Tijuana bender. There were still five steers bunched up on our side of the gate, bottlenecked, and they couldn't push through before the instinct to follow the herd overwhelmed them and they ran after the cows—outside the fence, of course, and toward the road.

Mark and I had a breathless consultation and decided that he should go with the cattle in the pasture. They were used to following his voice when he moved them to fresh pasture, so they might come to him, which would draw the loose steers back toward the barn. I was on plan B, trying to outflank the steers, get between them and the road, turn them, and drive them back along the fence and through the gate. There was no time to deliberate. I grabbed a big stick and ran. The steers got muddled in the stream and the trees and lost sight of the cows for a while, which gave me time to get around them and stake a position a few yards from the fence. Then they saw the cows again, rounding the corner of the pasture, and they barreled toward me.

I had learned some things by then about how to handle cattle, how a herd moves and why. To make yourself intimidating to them, I'd read, you must appear as large as possible and you must look at the animals directly, straight on with both eyes, as a predator would. You must be utterly confident that they will obey you, and under no circumstances should you show any doubt or fear. It is permissible to yell *"WHOA"* in a big, low voice, but shrieking would not be good. This is what I was thinking as the steers ran toward me, the biggest one in the lead, flanked by the rest in a tight arrow formation, and so I was standing firm and confident, feet planted wide, arms and stick outstretched, yelling *"WHOA"* in that big, low voice when the lead steer lowered his head and hit me.

It was the first time in my farm life that my experience as a high school cheerleader helped me. The steer hit me just below the hips, and as he lifted his head and tossed me in the air, I tucked my chin and piked. I believe I pulled a half gainer, because I landed sitting, slightly stunned but completely unhurt. The other steers stopped, staring. From the ground, in the sudden stillness, I could hear Mark calling the herd: "*Come* on, come *on*, Boss! *Come* on." The steers heard it, too, and so did the herd inside the fence, and, miraculously, they obeyed. I dusted myself off and followed them back across the ditch to the open gate, where the steers eagerly rejoined the herd.

We spent hours rebuilding the paddock, pounding new corner posts into the wet ground, constructing a laneway out of electric fence, and shuttling the herd through it. We managed to get the milking done and the horses fed before we stumbled to bed, but the steer we were meant to slaughter that day was spared for another week, and our restaurant lunch was a dead fantasy, gone as the day.

It was always something. Our baby turkeys arrived, and a murderous raccoon learned to jimmy the door to their brooder.

Then a pig went off its feed and stayed prostrate in the pigloo, covered in diamond-shaped spots. That was erysipelas, a disease that wasn't supposed to occur in our region but had been carried in by those turkey poults, which were shipped from the Midwest. Set those urgent needs against our puny human ones—like laundry, like dusting the furniture, like planning your upcoming wedding—and there was no contest. But if you are not careful, a farm can coerce you into thinking that you don't even have time to cook the very food you grow. There were weeks that spring when Mark and I would end our days so late and so exhausted we'd drive to town for a bag of chips and a pizza, one with a flabby crust and insipid sauce. I could live with dirty clothes, I was avoiding the wedding plans anyway, and, to be honest, I'd never been much of a duster of furniture, but if I wasn't going to get to eat our food, there was no point in going on. We had a come-to-Jesus meeting and agreed on that point, and from then on, we made it a priority to cook at least one good meal a day for ourselves, usually at midday. We also instituted and enforced a no-farming-on-Sundays rule. There were still chores and milking in the morning and evening, but the hours in between were set aside for human use, for being a couple.

Some Sundays I was desperate to get away from the farm and do something easy and familiar. My old pleasures were scarce. There were no cafés in town, no bookstores, no interesting little bars to discover. In the city, I'd averaged two movies a week. Here, the nearest movie theater was almost an hour away, stuck at the end of a mall next to a greasy food court, and the repertoire was a cycle of bad horror, bad high school comedy, and a children's movie. Still, every few Sundays, I'd get so hungry for entertainment I'd scrape the manure from my boots, force Mark into the car, and speed north. Mark loathes driving on principle, and he'd arrange his face into a faux tolerant expression and answer my questions with monosyllables to emphasize his sacrifice, but as soon as we were seated in the theater and the previews came on, he'd go slack-jawed, totally absorbed, no matter how terrible the fare. I realized that, unlike the rest of us, he had developed no immunity to a moving image. His parents didn't own a TV, and he hadn't seen much, filmwise, after *E.T.* You could prop him in front of the popcorn commercial and set it on a loop and he'd be riveted. It felt like a kind of defilement. I was the one who finally tired of the movies, which left me feeling empty on the long drive home.

The last old habit to fall away was shopping. I could feel the need to shop building up in me during the week, like an itch. I'm not talking about shopping for clothes, or shoes, or any of the other recreational kinds of shopping people generally do. I mean only the oddly comforting experience of flowing past shiny new merchandise, the everyday exchange of money for goods. In the city, most of the landscape is made up of objects for sale, and it's nearly impossible to leave your apartment without buying *something*—a newspaper, a cup of coffee, a bright bunch of Korean market flowers. When I went for days without buying anything, without setting eyes on commerce, without even starting the car to burn up some gas, I felt an achy withdrawal. The only shopping options within ten miles of the farm were a grocery store and a hardware store, and on

Sundays I'd visit the former and wheel a cart around the aisles, bathed in fluorescent light and Muzak. More and more often, though, I couldn't come up with anything we really needed, not a thing I really wanted, and the cart would remain empty until checkout, where I'd buy a copy of *People* and the thick, familiar pillow of the Sunday *New York Times*. More and more often I was happy to stay on the farm for our Sundays, walk the pastures with Mark, and fall back on our trusty old triumvirate of bed, stove, table.

We were trying to hammer out this big, awkward thing, bring it from theory into being. This idea we'd grabbed hold of—to create a farm that provided a whole diet to some as-yet-unknown number of annual subscribers, and meanwhile to revive the soul of this old piece of land—was either audacious or stupid, depending on your relationship to risk. It required building a wildly complex farm all at once, investing in multiple types of infrastructure. Mark's vegetable-growing experience was extensive, but our animal husbandry skills ran from thin to nonexistent. We were new to draft horses, knew nothing about horse-drawn machines, and had boxed ourselves into depending on them. As far as we knew, there was no precedent for this whole-diet model. We did not know how to price it, or if we could sell it. We had nothing to fall back on, had spent all our savings, the numbers shaved down so fine we could keep the balance in our heads. By the time the ground began to warm, it was somewhere in the mid–two figures. The farm we were working toward was only a figment, and it was a long shot, but we were both falling in love with it, in the way that parents love a baby even before it's born. I was the newcomer, the know-nothing, but I had never cared so much about anything in my life.

I was in love with the work, too, despite its overabundance. The world had always seemed disturbingly chaotic to me, my choices too bewildering. I was fundamentally happier, I found, with my focus on the ground. For the first time, I could clearly see the connection between my actions and their consequences. I knew why I was doing what I was doing, and I believed in it. I felt the gap between who I thought I was and how I behaved begin to close, growing slowly closer to authentic. I felt my body changing to accommodate what I was asking of it. I could lift the harness onto Sam's back without asphyxiating myself. I could carry two full five-gallon buckets with ease, tottering down the aisle of the barn like a Chinese peasant. I had always been attracted to the empty, sparkly grab bag of instant gratification, and I was beginning to learn something about the peace you can find inside an infinite challenge.

But why, oh, why, does passion always spawn conflict? As the farm began to take form, Mark and I argued fiercely over everything. We discovered that we had different desires, different fears, different visions for the farm. We were both way too stubborn. We lost whole precious daylight hours fighting over how to build a pig fence or whether the horses should spend the night inside or out. "But farming is my art," he would say finally, when we were both thoroughly frustrated and close to tears. That seemed ridiculously pretentious to me at first. How much further from art could we be, sweating and wallowing in the dirt like this? Later, after I'd been on many different farms and met many different farmers, I had to concede this point. A farm is a form of expression, a physical manifestation of the inner life of its farmers. The farm will reveal who you are, whether you like it or not. That's art. As a trump card, though, it was still junk. If this farm was art, then it was going to have to be a collaboration between equals.

I am a passive-aggressive disputant, happy to avoid the direct confrontation and tenderly nurse its grudge instead. Mark is a plain old tenacious arguer. He will grab hold of a disagreement and worry it, shaking it back and forth and back and forth until the crux of it drops out. That's why I know that those arguments were always about our two different basic fears. I was chiefly afraid of money—of poverty, of debt. It looked like our profit margin would be slim at best, and I thought that paying interest could enslave us. And if this thing failed, I did not want to be left to shovel out from under a pile of old bills. I had some experience with debt, and I had a deep fear of going back there. Mark, by contrast, had a friendly and lighthearted relationship with money, based in part on the fact that he has very little attachment to the having or not having of it. He could be happy living on a park bench, I told him. He did not disagree. But his history with money was actually much healthier than mine. He'd taken out a loan to start his farm in Pennsylvania, and he'd paid it back early. He had even saved enough from his paltry farm salaries to bail me out of the last part of my debt when I left the city for New Paltz. His fear was not of debt but of ruining ourselves with overwork. He'd seen it happen to other people, the farm gaining mass and speed until it ran over the farmer and squashed him. He worried that we would become so overwhelmed by work it would not be any fun anymore, or that his freedom to farm the way he wanted to would be limited. That freedom was worth more to him, he said, than so-called security. He was fond of quoting a farmer under whom he had apprenticed, who said that organic farms most commonly failed not from bankruptcy but from burnout or divorce. I wasn't sure about the former, but if we kept fighting like this, we were well on our way to the latter, and the wedding hadn't even happened yet.

One thing we had to agree on was that it was time to secure some members. We made up a flyer and posted it on the community board, in front of Town Hall. We were offering a full-diet share—including beef, pork, chicken, eggs, milk, vegetables, flours, grains, and dry beans, and our beautiful maple syrup—beginning the first week of August. It would take us until then to put all the pieces of the farm together, and to begin harvesting serious amounts of vegetables. Members who signed up before August could come to the farm each week to get their meat and milk, plus vegetables and other items as they became available. In the breath between the end of sugaring and the beginning of fieldwork, we shifted our focus to marketing.

We had some forces aligned against us on that front. We were new in this small, conservative town, a town that had watched good farms go under in the preceding decades. We were pitching a radical all-or-nothing, year-round membership model that was untried, even in the most agriculturally progressive pockets of the country. We were asking people to fork over thousands of dollars for the promise of a return that was by no means guaranteed. At the price we were charging, most people in our community couldn't afford to use our food as a supplement to their usual grocery store haul. They'd have to give up, like I had, that familiar and comforting experience of pushing a cart down an aisle. The central question in the kitchen would have to change from What do I want? to What is available? The time spent in the kitchen—in planning, in preparing, in cooking—would jump exponentially. Moreover, our frost-free growing season is only about a hundred days. To eat perishable food out of season, you have to make the time to can or freeze it while it is fresh and abundant. Those projects are fun and satisfying if you have the time for them, but if you're working a full-time job while trying to satisfy the needs of your children, they begin to seem sweaty and tedious. Maybe most important, farm food itself is totally different from what most people now think of as food: none of those colorful boxed and bagged products, precut, parboiled, ready to eat, and engineered to appeal to our basest desires. We were selling the opposite: naked, unprocessed food, two steps from the dirt.

I knew, from what I was experiencing in our kitchen, that if we could get people to take a taste, some things we were producing would sell themselves. You could not have a pork chop from one of our pastured pigs and ever want to go back to the factory-raised kind. Same with our eggs, with their bright orange yolks standing at attention in the pan. But other things would be a harder sell. Our grass-fed beef was tastier but much tougher than the corn-fattened beef Americans are used to. We experimented with hanging the sides in the cooler for three, four, or even five weeks before butchering. This gave the meat a buttery texture but also a high flavor that I absolutely relished but some people found unpleasant. Also, we were talking about whole animals, and for reasons both ethical and economic, we needed to make use of every part, from tongue to testicles. We'd be asking people to eat things they couldn't identify and didn't know how to cook. We found, from giving away samples, that the rich, flavorful Jersey milk I loved so much was just too different from the store-bought kind for some palates to accept, especially if they were used to drinking low-fat or skim. Moreover, we couldn't offer the kind of consistency that consumers have come to expect from grocery store food. Could we really expect people to change their habits so radically, and pay good money for it?

In our favor, we had Mark, who, after all, had convinced me to leave everything I knew behind and join him, using only the strength of his own conviction. He believed in the farm we were creating with at least as much force as he believed in our relationship, and when he believes in something, it is contagious, the gift of all good salesmen. At his farm in Pennsylvania, he'd developed what we now call his drug-dealer method of marketing, which meant giving lots of things away, getting people to try a bite of something, anything, knowing that it was so good they'd be hooked and come back. When the growing season began he would stand at the intersection in town with a crate of produce and push heads of lettuce on the passing motorists.

We had lucky timing. We arrived in Essex just as the wave of localism was gathering and words like *foodshed* were heard for the first time. Chefs and food writers were drawing attention to the quality of food produced by small-scale farmers. The idea of organics had already penetrated into the mainstream, even in the hinterlands. We fielded a small but steady trickle of inquiries from people who wanted to know where their food was coming from, wanted food free from hormones and antibiotics, food whose origins they could see with their eyes. Another part of our community—truly local folks of a certain age—could care less about buzzwords, but they were already familiar with the taste of farm-raised, local food, because that was the food they'd grown up on, and they missed it.

What made it work were the people in our little town. They embraced us. I felt they had been watching us, through the fall and winter, to see if we were serious. They had been friendly but had reserved judgment. That spring, they watched us dig in and struggle, and they saw that we weren't fooling around. They thought of themselves as underdogs, far from the busy and powerful places of the world, so small they were often forgotten. When we became part of them, I think they felt it was their duty to support us, underdog to underdog. Some became members, others helped us in different ways, with tools or advice, by joining us for a few hours at chores. A few became regulars. Liz Wilson began coming over on Fridays to wash the milk jars and make us lunch. Our neighbors John and Katharine came once a week, too, to clean out the barn, or move bales of hay, or whatever heavy work was on the top of our list. Thomas LaFountain helped with butchering when we got behind, even if his own cooler was full of carcasses awaiting his knife and saw. The Owenses came when an animal was sick or hurt. Don Hollingsworth, one of the white-haired people who had made us welcome at the church potluck back in the fall, was a master woodworker, and he would take our broken wooden things to his shop and return them whole, better than new. Shane Sharpe came over, alone or with Luke, to guide us past the problems that stymied us in the machine shop. All he wanted in return, when everything was put back together and running smoothly, was a beer and someone to drink it with.

Lars bought the first two shares. He lived four hours south of us, and we all knew they were pity shares and he would not get his money's worth. Then Barbara Kunzi knocked on the door. She'd farmed a few miles from our place for sixteen years, until a string of drought years dried up her well and compelled her to sell the farm and move to town. She knew her pitchforks from her plum tomatoes and had every reason to doubt the soundness of our venture, but she sat down at our kitchen table and wrote us a check. By the time the ground was thawed we had seven members, and our bank account did not ring quite as hollow when we made a deposit.

That little pad of money, small as it was, seemed to soften the tension between Mark and me. With members to provide food for, we had new direction and a clear joint purpose. Every Friday evening from four until seven, our members would come to pick up their shares. No matter what else happened during the week—injuries, stampedes, disasters—we had to pull it together on Friday and get food out to the members.

The first week, we set up a bare-bones sort of store at the

front of the farm, in one of the newer structures, a three-sided pavilion with a good concrete floor. All we had to offer was milk, meat, and eggs, quarts of our first maple syrup, which were very popular, and white jars of lard, which went untouched. Mark decided lard needed rebranding and became a lard evangelist. The next week he talked up its health benefits and its culinary virtues, then he began giving out samples of lard-based pie crusts and vegetables sautéed in lard. Before spring was over, lard was in high demand.

I don't like to think of how many laws were broken at those early distributions. We did not yet have a milk house, or a dairy license, or even a dedicated refrigerator. We did not yet have a butcher shop. Mark hacked up sides of beef or pork to order, out in the open, glancing quickly at the illustrations in our worn paperback copy of *Basic Butchering of Livestock and Game*. Even then, though, our members brought a happy, jovial atmosphere with them, arriving with baskets and boxes and bags empty, leaving with them full. Most of them were already friends with one another, and those who weren't quickly became so, bonding over stories of the meals they'd made that week, over recipes and storage tips. It was fun, like hosting a weekly cocktail party at a third-world market.

The early improvements came through our nearest neighbors, John and Dot Everhart, who were retired farmers, married sixty years. They'd managed a dairy south of us for decades, until the place—a beautiful spread on the lake—was sold as a second home. The story we'd heard in town was that the new owners offered to let the Everharts stay on at the farm out of deference to the number of years they'd been there. The only catch was that John would have to give up his guns. The Everharts quietly picked up and moved, to a neat new modular home across the street from us.

John checked in on us every few days, coming up the driveway in his truck or across the fields on his ATV, Dot on the back. He was a wealth of the kind of granular knowledge you can get only from a lifetime of farming in one place. Mark peppered him with questions about the timing of planting and plowing, weather patterns, soil and forage types, our local predators. Like Shep Shields, John had farmed with horses as a young man, but unlike Shep he was no fan of them, and it made him nervous to see a woman driving them. He worried I'd get hurt. "Hot team you got there," he said disapprovingly. He disliked our Sam in particular. "You know, best thing to do with that high-headed horse is shoot him."

John worked at the dump just up the street from us. Almost everyone in town visits the dump once a week, and it is the closest thing we have to a social center. John kept his eyes open for us and put aside things that he thought we could use. He brought us a large upright freezer and a good-size refrigerator, both slightly dinged but not too old and perfectly usable. He brought us tables and shelving until Mark and I decided our pavilion no longer looked like a third-world market. It looked like a second-world market at least.

By the end of April our first seeds were well up, in rows of soil-filled flats on the farmhouse's sunny, glassed-in porch. We'd planted the onions between sap runs in March, and now we had ten thousand small, green, bladelike sprouts striving to grow. Leeks came next, and then herbs, broccoli, pepper, tomato, flowers, lettuce—five types—cabbage, and kale. I'd begun to understand what *farm scale* meant. Seeding was like running a small, muddy factory. The potting soil we used came in a one-ton sack ("If it weighs a ton," my friend Alexis said when she heard this, "can you still call it a sack?"). We stirred water into batches of the potting soil until a handful of it would drip once or twice when you squeezed it in your hand. We borrowed a soil blocker, a nifty metal mold on a stick, from some neighbor farmers and used it to form the moist soil into cubes. Into the center of each cube we dropped seeds, some so small you had to squint to see them. Then we dusted the tops of the flats with more potting soil and watered them. I loved that miniature work in the pale spring light. I liked imagining what the seeds would become, and I liked the contrast with the usual farm jobs, which always seemed to involve heavy lifting.

The nights were still dangerously cold for tender young seedlings. When the weather radio warned of freezing temperatures, we opened the windows between the house and the porch and stoked up the woodstove. We bought box fans to push the warmer air around. The porch got so crowded with flats, maneuvering among them for watering was like playing a game of Twister. Then we ran out of room entirely. The tomatoes placed in the porch's corners were not getting enough light, and they were growing too tall and thin. We stacked hay bales into rectangles on the farmhouse lawn and topped them with windows John found for us at the dump: poor-man's cold frames. We moved our leggy tomatoes outside and crossed our fingers.

Mark was not used to working with ad hoc systems like this. On his farm in Pennsylvania, the start-up phase had been funded by a twenty-thousand-dollar loan, which had allowed him to buy all the equipment he needed and also build a greenhouse. Because of my fear of debt, and because this whole-diet farm venture was new and untested, we'd agreed to get through our first trial year on nothing but our savings. Since those were already spent by planting time, we were bootstrapping, and sometimes we went too far. We didn't buy a $250 garden cart—a tool so basic and essential to the everyday work of hauling heavy things on a farm, I now can't imagine how we did without it—until the middle of our second season. We did not have enough hoses, which meant spending scarce time unhooking and dragging them from one place to another, or else hauling loaded buckets. And with the thrown-together cold frames, we made a bad miscalculation. When the plants were good-size seedlings, the temperature dipped unexpectedly low one night, and in the morning we found all them drooping, tender leaves and stems turned the darker green of frost-nipped death. It was too late, by then, to start again, and buying started plants did not fit into our budget.

We were saved by a fellow farmer, Beth Spaugh. She had left her job as county extension agent several years earlier because, she said, God told her to farm. She'd turned the small acreage around her house into a market garden and chicken coop, and, through faith, hard work, and sheer stubbornness, carved out a niche for herself selling vegetables and eggs at the local farmers' markets. When she heard about our frozen tomatoes, she drove over to our place with her truck bed full of stocky, vibrant tomato plants. She'd planted extra, she said, and these were her leftovers. She knew we had no money, so she gave them to us for free.

We found that kind of generosity over and over again our first year. Without it, I don't think the farm could have survived. Gifts were made quietly, so as not to embarrass us. When Billy Shields came over to artificially inseminate our cow Raye, he refused to take a check for it. When we pressed him, he looked away. "I like to help a young farmer just starting out," he said, and that was the end of the discussion. I knew that Thomas LaFountain stored our meat in his cooler at a cut rate, and I suspected that our vet, Dr. Goldwasser, was undercharging us for farm calls. The next spring, when we still did not have a greenhouse, our neighbors to the north, Mike and Laurie Davis, let us use theirs, even though they started their own CSA that year, which made us their direct competitors.

Beth Spaugh's tomato plants thrived in our cold frames, and by the time the threat of frost was over, they were covered in little yellow blossoms. In the trip between her farm and ours, the plants had lost their identification tags, so when we planted them in the field, the many varieties were all mixed together—slicing tomatoes intermingled with cherry tomatoes, and hollow tomatoes meant for stuffing growing next to a bright yellow variety that looks cheekily similar to a peach. We'd never again have such a wildly beautiful tomato patch, and it produced extraordinarily well, as though even the plants themselves were inclined to help us when they could.

*   *   *

Don't let anyone tell you that growing vegetables is not a violent act. The muted sound of a plow tearing through roots is almost obscene, like the sound of a fist meeting flesh. Before planting, we had to raze the ground.

Plowing is primary tillage, the first and crudest step in making ground ready for seed. It takes tremendous power. Imagine digging a ditch nine inches wide, six inches deep, and eleven miles long. That's what it takes to plow a single acre. The job of the plow is to rip through the earth and then to flip it over, so that the surface is buried. There are plows for breaking new ground and plows for stubble, for hills, for clay, muck, and sand. The simplest horse-drawn kind is the one-bottom walking plow, a heavy pointed hunk of steel with handles on the back end, a clevis to hitch to the horses on the front. When a walking plow is well-made and properly adjusted, and the horses are fit and well-trained, plowing is pure pleasure. The plow floats through the soil, and the furrow opens up behind you in a long dark wave. Our first plow was an ancient relic that Shep Shields had loaned us, found in the back of his barn. It was a rusty thing with cracked handles, and its share, the curved metal piece that turns the ground, was badly worn. It was missing its coulter, the sharp knife that is supposed to slice through the sod in front of the share. Our first attempt to use that monster was an abject failure.

Sam and Silver had not worked hard for three weeks, since the end of sugar season. Meanwhile, they'd been eating grain and the first green tips of the growing grass, which gave them the energy of kindergarteners after too much cake. We loaded the sorry-looking plow onto our stone boat and set out for the back of the farm. There was a ten-acre piece that had been rented out to another farmer to grow corn the year before, and the soil there was loose. We weren't planning to use it that year, so we thought it would be a good place to practice before we attempted to open up the thick sod in the fields we wanted for our vegetables.

In the old paintings, the plowman is alone. He holds the handles of the plow, one in each hand, and steers the horses with the lines knotted around his shoulders. We were barely competent driving horses with two hands, let alone with our shoulders, so we decided to split the job in two. I guided the horses, and Mark handled the plow. I had the slightly better end of the deal, because I could keep clear of the plow handles, while Mark kept getting whacked by them, right in the gut. Sam was hitched on the right, the so-called furrow horse, charged with walking in the soft dirt of his newly dug ditch, keeping a straight line. He understood his job and stayed in the right place, but the plow would not behave. It plunged deep into the loose soil and made the horses strain against their collars, and then it surfed upward and popped out of the soil entirely, and the horses lurched forward against nothing. There were almost no rocks in that field, but when we were unlucky enough to connect with one, the plow stopped dead. Then we had to back the horses up, dragging the heavy plow by hand to the last clean place in the furrow, or else come out of the furrow entirely, circle around, and begin again.

Mark was certain that whatever was going wrong was my

fault. The horses were moving too fast, and he wanted me to slow them down, but they were high on grain and didn't want to work at such a slow pace. They pulled at their bits until my arms felt stretched to apelike length. When Mark wanted me to move the horses a fraction of an inch to the right he'd say, "Right!" but he wouldn't give me time to react before saying "Right!" again, and then I'd be too far right and he would be barking "Left!" Before we finished a whole furrow I wanted to kill him. (If I could have glimpsed the future, this is what I would have seen: Late spring, sunny afternoon, me seven months pregnant with our daughter, driving the team for Mark while he plowed, not because we needed two people for the job by then but for the pure pleasure of it, the knowing horses doing their work and the plow moving smoothly through soil and we two humans enjoying it like other couples enjoy a waltz together. But that was far in the future, with a lot of trying in between.)

We kept at it doggedly for half a morning before we admitted it was hopeless. We had only a small window of dry early spring weather, and at the rate we were going, it would take us about a year to turn the five acres we needed.

We hired our neighbor Paul and his big tractor with a five-bottom plow, and in a matter of a couple hours he opened up our vegetable ground, five acres in five fields on the good soil that ran parallel to the road. I walked behind him, in the furrow, in awe of the tractor's gargantuan tires, the deep throb of the engine, mesmerized by the destructive power of the plow hitched behind. At the end of each row he lifted it, and the five shares, scoured by the earth, flashed like swords. He made the turn and they sank into the ground again, and the soft, grassy surface of the earth—its variegated pad of flora and fauna—was replaced by wave after wave of raw soil. The seagulls flocked knowingly to the sound of the tractor. At the bottoms of the furrows, the shocked worms writhed and dove for cover.

We gave the new places their civilized names: Home Field, next to the farmhouse. Pine Field, tucked between two groves of trees. Mailbox Field, at the end of our long driveway. Monument Field, where the best soil was, named for an obelisklike rock that stood alongside it. Small Joy, carved out of a hayfield and flanked by a stream. Each field was an acre, more or less. I could see the fresh furrows from the upstairs window, red in the last late light.

The next morning, Mark and I walked the headlands, counting steps, taking measure. The land was subdued but not yet entirely broken. Plowing loosens the topsoil and buries sod, but it leaves a rough surface. In our new fields, the sod and the soil clung to their old form, standing up in those dark waves, leaning on each other to make a range of tiny peaks. Stray tufts of grass stuck out between them. Smoothing the seedbed is what the harrow is for. Ancient-sounding word with its connotations of distress.

There was a disc harrow on the farm, but it was the modern kind, humongous, meant to be pulled by a large tractor. Luckily, Shane Sharpe had loaned us his horse-drawn disc harrow. The day after we plowed, Mark and I rolled it onto the driveway and hitched Sam and Silver to it. It was a simple machine, a six-foot-long metal frame that rolled along on a dozen slightly cupped metal discs. The discs were divided into two gangs, their relationship to each other adjustable, so that when traveling on the farm roads, they rolled along in one straight line, but in the field they could be angled toward one another to form a V. The discs cut into the surface of the soil, further loosening it and breaking up clods. Each disc throws some soil inward, to flatten out lumps and furrows, and kill weeds. There was a hard metal tractor seat bolted onto the top of the frame, and a crude metal rack behind, to hold rocks for added weight.

I took to the disc harrow immediately. Harrowing with it was a more reasonable job than plowing for a teamster as inexperienced as I was. If the horses and I couldn't manage to travel in a perfectly straight line, we left an interesting trail behind us but didn't jeopardize the whole operation. I relaxed, and so did the horses, who seemed calmed by the steady pull. It was quiet in Small Joy, except for the crazy pinging call of a bobolink and the faint, far-off sound of a rooster. Nico, who'd followed us, matched the horses' pace with her shepherdy slink. She raised her ears at a killdeer that was desperately trying to make her chase it, flopping around with her wing out, close to the ground. I guess we'd wrecked the bird's nest with the plow the day before. I tried for a minute to imagine a way of eating that involves no suffering and came down to Thoreau next to the pond with his little patch of beans. Then I remembered that he walked to his mother's house in town every day for lunch.

The furrows smoothed and flattened out behind us. When I stopped to clear a stick from between the discs, the ground felt springy underneath my feet, like a giant trampoline. It was a good workout for the horses, who were out of shape after their time off. We stopped at the end of each pass for a rest, and they stood and blew, and the sweat dripped from their bellies onto the raw earth like a balm or a blessing.

In May, it felt like spring was accelerating, under the influence of more and more sun. There was no time for social engagements now; phone calls went unreturned. Our attention was focused on the land and its changing rhythm. I rode Sam to the other side of the farm in the evenings, to check the beef herd, count heads. Each trip, I saw some new species budding or blooming or being born. In the woods, first the trillium, then the trout lily, the wild strawberries, and the violets. One night the plum trees in our neighbor's orchard were snowy with blossoms. Then the gnarled old apple trees in the sugar bush— ancient relics of some other farmer's plans—thrust out their tender leaves.

As soon as the disc harrowing was finished, a bank of slate-colored clouds moved in and it began to rain, cold and steady. Mark and I walked along the edges of the fields and watched the rivulets form, the topsoil washing down the slightest rise into miniature deltas. The time for seeding and transplanting had arrived, but we couldn't get into the fields when they were wet like that. We'd crush the life out of the soil, push out the air spaces that plants like so much, turn the seedbed into concrete. Making breakfast, I watched out the window, nervous, waiting for the weather to shift.

My old friend James, when he sees a pretty girl, calls her

foxy. A really pretty girl is *fox factor five*. That's what I thought of, looking out the kitchen window at the May rain, when the fox ran through the pasture. I could not help but admire her. She moved lightly across the ground, fox-trotting, her tail carried like a banner. Her fur looked as though she had just had it washed, conditioned, and blown out at the salon. I ran to the next window, watching, then realized that the chickens had wandered far out into the pasture, scratching the wet ground for the worms. And sure enough, the fox was tugging at something in the grass, something half as heavy as she was: a fat black hen, one of our best layers. The fox probably had kits to feed. A real farmer would have gone for the gun. I knew that, but I couldn't bear the thought of tattering her. I rallied the dog and ran out of the house in my slippers, gave a war cry that raised the fur on Nico's back and sent her across the field at what passes for a run in a thirteen-year-old dog with bad hips. The fox melted into the landscape, and I was left in the rain with wet feet and a dead chicken.

We spent a wet day at the kitchen table, with a map of our new fields and a list of the crops we were planning to grow. We'd ordered extra seed, enough to plant three or four times the produce we estimated we'd need. That was our insurance, in case the weather was bad, crops failed, the membership grew, or all three. We'd decided to go heavy on the no-nonsense crops that most people eat regularly, not try to get too fancy. And we were feeding people through the long North Country winter, so we would need a whole lot of roots. If we did well and had extra, we could always feed it to the cows or pigs.

We filled in the map of Monument Field with rows of potatoes, cabbage, kale, onions and leeks, collards, carrots, beets. Dry beans, winter squash, and popcorn would cluster together in Pine Field, next to melons and the tomatoes. We'd put the early crops in Small Joy: peas, spinach, the first plantings of radish and lettuce. After those crops were harvested, we'd plant the field to winter wheat. Home Field would be reserved for flowers and herbs.

It looked like a real farm, on paper at least. Outside in the real world, it was still too wet to plant. At least the rain hustled the green into the pastures. The dairy cows were enjoying a flush of new clover. Delia had come to us already pregnant, artificially inseminated at the Shields farm, and she was due to calve at the end of May. We'd stopped milking her eight weeks earlier, to give her a rest. Just before we dried her off, she had been looking awfully skinny, her hip bones jutting out sharply, ribs showing. The calf was growing inside of her. At her last milking, my cheek against her flank, I could feel it move. Delia was putting her energy into the calf and into milk—more even than she was taking in from her food. "She's milkin' off her back," Neal Owens said when he saw her. Some cows are like that, too generous for their own good. The two-month rest and the new grass had done a lot for her. She'd put on flesh, and by the time she was ready to calve, she looked about as good as a cow can look without ears. I had her due date written in red on the calendar, and I read and reread the chapter on calving in *The Family Cow* and watched for the signs of imminence—a ballooning udder, a puffy vulva, and depressions in the flesh on either side of the root of her tail, which would mean the calf was moving toward the birth canal.

It was raining, of course, the night she calved. When I'd gone to get Raye at milking time that evening, Delia had been off by herself, not grazing, her bag stretched so tight the teats stood out taut, like four fingers on a blown-up rubber glove. She looked too heavy to move, so I left her alone and walked Raye in by herself.

I checked Delia at midnight, and she was lying quietly at the edge of the pasture. I set the alarm for three but woke before it went off and nudged Mark, who got up and pulled on his clothes. (These days, neither of us would be quite so vigilant. Sleep is too precious, our cows have always birthed without difficulty, and they seem to prefer to do so in solitude. But this was our first birth, and we were excited and a little anxious.) Outside, the rain was steady but the air was still, and it wasn't cold. Two of the cats joined us at the barn, scampering in front of us like sprites.

In the pasture, we heard the low, urgent grunt—so familiar to me now—that a new mother cow makes, the sound of bovine tenderness. In the light from my headlamp the cats' eyes gleamed. I scanned the field, looking for the source of the sound. I saw another pair of eyes—Raye—then another pair—Delia—and then, finally, on the ground, a third. Closer, we could make out Delia with her head down, licking her little prize anxiously, intently. The calf struggled to stand, and Delia made encouraging sounds. Raye mooed, too, maybe remembering, in her slow bovine way, her own last calf. The little one wobbled to its feet, sure of where it was supposed to go but unable to make its new legs obey. Delia seemed to know she was supposed to do something, too, but was hoping for God's sake it had nothing to do with the very sore, swollen balloon underneath her. Every time the calf lurched toward the udder, Delia turned away, so they were moving in a drunken circle. Raye watched, interested, but kept a polite distance. I came closer, peeked under the calf's tail, and saw the tiny vertical slit of the vulva. A heifer then. Mark and I smiled at each other in the dark.

The barnyard upends the cruel calculus of human cultures that prize male babies and devalue females. On a farm, one male's worth of sperm is enough to service a score or more of females. Extra testosterone is a liability. It only causes problems: fights, injuries to animals, injuries to humans, broken fences, unintended breedings. In the milking herds, the rule is ironclad. Most dairy bull calves are slaughtered young, for veal. As bulls, dairy cattle are unpredictable, dangerous as loaded guns. As steers, they grow up stringy and thin, not muscly, and on most farms, it doesn't pay to raise them for meat. The birth of a bull calf in the dairy herd is always tinged with sadness.

A heifer is a different story, a cause for celebration. If all went well, this calf would be with us for years, an intimate, practically a member of the family. She'd get the best hay, the best grass, the best winter quarters. The trade-off would be that when she was in her mother's place, tenderly licking clean a new baby, she would not get to keep hers, either.

This calf would need only a gallon of milk per day, and Delia would be giving several times that amount. If we left them together, the calf would get too much milk, and we would get too little. Some farms will leave mamas and babies together for a few hours a day, separating them for a long stretch before milkings, but we didn't have the time or the infrastructure to do that. We'd decided to put Delia back out with Raye and bottle-feed the calf. Since we were going to separate them, the sooner the better, before they could bond.

Mark wrapped a towel around the heifer, hoisted her onto his shoulders, front legs in his left hand, hind legs in his right, and walked toward the barn. We expected Delia to follow, but she couldn't understand where her calf had gone. She nosed the grass where she had given birth, wondering if it was still there but invisible. She bawled urgently and would not move from the spot. Raye, though, seemed to think it must be milking time and was happy to head toward the barn. And then Delia came, too, and I followed her, so that we made a funny little parade through the rainy night. Delia's hind legs swung wide around her swollen bag, and she trailed a little string of gore.

As soon as she was moving, Delia stopped bawling for her calf. From then on, it was as though there had never been a calf, or she had willed herself to forget.

The cows walked into their usual stanchions. Mark had put fresh, tender hay in front of both of them, and a bucket of warm water with a little salt in it for Delia. She sucked it down in gulps. In the light I could see her bag more clearly. Milk beaded at the tips of her teats. There was the fleshy, iron smell of birth, richer than blood. The cats bounced down the aisle, hopeful, and then bounced away. Delia nibbled some hay and then paused, her gaze turned inward, and the little piece of gore hanging out her back end made some progress, then retreated. That was the afterbirth, which Neal Owens had called cleanings. It was supposed to be expelled in the hour or two after calving.

Mark settled the calf in the nursery we'd made by filling the shed next to the house with a thick layer of straw, and she promptly went to sleep. I washed Delia's udder and grasped her teats. She was so swollen, I could fit only two fingers on them. Still, the colostrum spilled from her, the color and thickness of eggnog. This is the first milk, full of the mother's antibodies. It would give the calf passive immunity to disease until her own immune system kicked in. Curious, I tasted it. It was salty and a little bitter, nothing like milk and not something I'd want to try again. Once I had a quart in my bucket, Mark filled a calf bottle and went to feed the heifer. A calf's gut can absorb those crucial antibodies for only the first twenty-four hours after birth. The more colostrum she got, and soon, the stronger her resistance to disease would be while she was small and vulnerable. If she got none, she would die.

The great big, taut bag softened a little as I milked, and Delia seemed grateful. She looked at me with patient eyes, as though I were her missing calf. I felt her heave, and the afterbirth came partway out and hung there. I could see the meaty cotyledons, where the placenta had been attached to Delia's uterus, and the cellophane layers of the calf's sac. Another heave and it was delivered, perhaps fifteen pounds of it. Delia strained in her stanchion, trying to get at it. I moved the dripping heap to her head, and she reached for it, chewing, slurping, chewing, slurping until it was gone, leaving her vegetarian's mouth disconcertingly bloody. I don't know why new mothers' inner compasses tell them to do this, whether it's to keep the wolves away or to fill the newly empty gut, but I do know that someone should make a horror film about it.

When Delia was milked and both cows were back on pasture, the sun was up. Mark went to bed, to get a few minutes of rest before the real day started. I stopped to inspect the calf, who was curled into the straw. She was fawn-colored with a nip of white above a back hoof so fresh from its long bath it was perfectly clean and soft, the bottom still rough, like a brand-new shoe with a crepe rubber sole. White spots on her flanks, like her mother, but the continents rearranged: Australia on her right side, Greenland on her left. Her pretty deer's head was capped with translucent ears. She extended her rear legs, then rested, showing me the four pink nubbins that would become her teats. She unfolded her front legs cautiously, one at a time, and wobbled there. Her focus seemed to shift between this new world and the quiet within. She was still only tenuously connected to our side, to light and time, air and gravity. At births, I find that it's this, and not the slip and splash of delivery, that gives us a glimpse of mystery. Newly born creatures carry the great calm of the Before with them, for minutes or hours, and when you are close to it, you can feel it, too.

I named her June. For weeks, when I fell into bed exhausted, Mark had been telling me, "You think this is busy? Just wait until June." When I was too tired to finish dinner, he would nudge the plate at me gently. "Eat," he'd say. "You'll need it come June." I gathered that, on a Venn diagram of the year's work, June was the space where everything intersected. There'd still be planting to do, and harvesting would have begun in earnest, and with the long hours of sunlight, the weeds would be going nuts. There would be hay to think about, too, and the pastures growing rank. Maybe I named the little calf June to tame the idea of it, to make it less threatening, or maybe to impart to her the vigor of it, the vital energy of the solstice.

At morning milking, Delia looked dopey. I consulted with Mark, and we decided that she was probably tired out from labor, and that we should keep an eye on her. When I went out to the pasture later that morning to move the cows' fence, she looked much worse. I took her by the collar and tried to bring her into the barn, but she stumbled and fell and could not get back up. She felt horribly cold, as though she were already mostly dead. I ran to the house and called Dr. Goldwasser. He was out on a farm call, would come as soon as he could.

I went back to the pasture and sat with Delia. She was curled up like her calf had been, forelegs tucked, head curved around toward her flank, with her nose resting on the ground. She looked ready for the journey back into the dark. I watched for her breaths, which I could barely see, shallow and slow. There were a million things on my to-do list, but I couldn't bear to leave her. I went to the house, got the latest issue of *The New Yorker*, and read articles to her out loud.

Dr. Goldwasser arrived an hour later, coming across the pasture with his bag of tricks. "She's got milk fever," he said. He touched her eyeball, and its lid barely flinched. "She's pretty far gone." Milk fever is not a fever at all but a deadly metabolic imbalance that afflicts some dairy cows at calving. Jerseys are especially prone. Their milk comes in abundantly, drawing calcium from the blood faster than the blood can recruit more from its storage place, in the bones. The level of calcium in the blood drops. Without sufficient blood calcium levels, muscles cannot function. Paralysis sets in, limbs, lungs, heart.

In his calm, easy way, Dr. Goldwasser rocked Delia's weight onto her folded knees so he could lift her head and put a rope halter around it. He found the thick vein in her neck where the blood was still coursing, slow and sluggish, and pushed his needle in. He hooked the rubber tubing to a plastic bottle of calcium and held it low. "Not too fast," he said. "Too fast and you give them heart failure." I felt Delia tremble, and I thought she was finally dying. "No, that's a good thing," said Dr. Goldwasser. "That means it's working." By the time the bottle was empty, the trembling had become a deep, strong shiver. He hooked up another bottle, let it drip slowly into her. When the second bottle was empty, she struggled to her feet, looking as stunned as Lazarus. She shook for another hour, the muscles working to bring back the warmth of life, but long before she stopped shivering she was grazing again, her bovine equanimity restored. If she'd seen anything at the brink of death, it wasn't startling enough to make her lose her appetite.

A south wind blew all night, and the next morning the sun came up bright in a cloudless, robin-egg sky. It gained strength as it rose, drew the water from the dark surfaces of the fields, firming them, warming them. The weather held, and two days later, Mark and I toured our five plowed acres. The high parts of the fields were dry, but in the low parts, water still gathered in puddles, and our feet sank. The weather radio called for more rain at the end of the week, and the plants waiting on the porch and in our cold frames were yellowing, straining against the confines of their small dirt cells. We decided to risk smoothing the seedbed with the spring-tine harrow, the final step before marking our rows and planting.

The feeling you get when you step out of the barn with a team of horses on a morning like that is so specific and so bright there ought to be a name for it. I hooked Sam and Silver to the spring-tine harrow, a simple frame with C-shaped tines that stick down into the soil to loosen the top layer, level it, knock out clumps. There's no seat on the spring-tine harrow. You get to walk behind.

We walked down the driveway, past Home Field and Mailbox. The fields were already showing the personalities they'd keep for as long as they remained in existence. Home Field had good drainage and beautiful loamy soil, but its placement was awkward, abutting a grove of trees, which made it difficult to turn the horses at the end of a row. Mailbox was easier to maneuver in, but it contained a big streak of clay. After a rain the clay would clump around the horses' feet, and stay heavy and too wet until it suddenly cracked at the surface like old porcelain and was too hard and too dry.

We pulled up in Monument Field, where our potatoes were scheduled to go. Our neighbor Ron had told us that a house had once stood at the edge of this field. The plow had revealed several of its broken bricks. This land had been farmed since before the American Revolution. The stock, the crops, the fence lines, the buildings, and the farmers had come and gone, passing over the fields like shadows in the course of the day. You can't truly own a farm, no matter what the deed says. It has a life of its own. You can love it beyond measure, and you are responsible for it, but at most you're married to it. I levered the tines into the surface of the soil. The horses pushed into their collars and moved forward with energy. It felt good to walk along behind them, smelling the spring smells of good, damp earth and warm horses.

We'd finished half the field when I heard the tines clank against something metal. I whoaed the horses and stooped to pick it up. It was a horseshoe, crusted with rust and dirt. One bent nail was fused to it, hand-forged. It was just about the size of my hand with all my fingers spread. If they wore them, Sam and Silver would require shoes the size of dinner plates. The old-time farm horses were smaller, tough and compact, closer to one thousand pounds than to our two-thousand-pound giants. I wondered what that old horse was up to the day he lost his shoe. It might have been a day like that day, when the low end of the field was still too wet to work, and they were out working anyway because the planting needed to be done, or the weeds were threatening to get away. I thought of the farmer who drove the horse, the man or boy who would have appreciated the rockless, forgiving soil like I did, the kind of soil, I knew, that most farmers only dream of. I thought of him looking around for that shoe after realizing his horse had cast it, the dark ribbon of iron blending in with the dirt. Then giving up, going in to dinner, his horseshoe waiting all these years under the surface, an irrelevance to all the farmers who came between us, for me to find it, and imagine him.

*   *   *

Mark was still courting me. His love and his commitment never wavered, even though mine seemed to go up and down like an EKG. The gifts that he brought me that spring were humble and so beautiful. The contrast between the harshness of our lives then and the tenderness of those small gestures was shocking. A little bundle of wildflowers, laid on my pillow in the afternoon. A small drawing of the hawk we'd watched flying low over the marshy field behind the house. After the plants were in the ground I went to bed with a fever, and he brought me a plate of wild strawberries ringed by flowers and leaves, and sat on the edge of my bed and chattered and joked while I ate them, and would not take any for himself.

When my fever was gone, there was a big hunger in its place. There were no greens yet in the cultivated fields, but my body had begun to request them. Politely at first, and then not so much. It's not bleak winter that is meager on our farm but bright spring. We walked through the pastures with a basket and a pair of kitchen shears. The wild greens had the jump on the season. Mark cut some young stinging nettles from the rich soil at the edges of the barnyard. He cut piles of the ubiquitous dandelion, with its tonic, bitter leaves. I was ravenous for them.

Every season has its delicacy, even the skimpiest one. Our butter at the end of spring is the best of the year. The pastures are at their finest, and the cows are in heaven, filling their bellies with the fast-growing grass, not yet molested by flies, the weather cool and breezy. The butter that comes from the cows then is soft, luscious, and the deep, vibrant color of antique gold.

Mark threw a big, bright hunk of that butter into a heated pot, added a diced onion and, when it had gone limp, a big pile of the dark green nettles. They wilted immediately, which took away their sting, and the smell of them was very green, like spinach but without the acridity and with a wild, nutty edge. He added some garlic, then some chicken stock, and a few handfuls of rice, and let it simmer until the greens and the rice were soft. He added salt and pepper and a scrape of nutmeg, blended it smooth, and served it with a dollop of sour cream on top, a hunk of his good bread on the side. The dandelion greens went into the still-hot pan for a few moments. Dressed with a little oil and a splash of good balsamic vinegar, they were a tart sidekick to the nourishing nettle soup.

The members were hungry for greens, too, even if they were only weeds. We found the best patches of nettles and lamb's-quarter on the farm and harvested big bushels of them.

Meanwhile, I was on a campaign to sell the idea of scrapple, a food that Mark had introduced me to, via his Amish friends in Pennsylvania. I thought it was the most ingenious and delicious breakfast item I'd ever eaten. I had made about a hundred pounds of it when we'd last slaughtered a pig, and I was having a hard time moving it. I thought maybe our members just didn't know what it was or how it was made, so I wrote this note, my own attempt at rebranding, to the members.

Don't knock it just because it sounds like a cross between *scrap* and *offal*! Scrapple is fine dining. Take bones of one pig plus any meat that hasn't been used for cuts or sausage and simmer until the meat is free of bones. Remove bones. Pass broth and meat through a grinder. Bring to a boil, and add fine meal (corn or wheat or buckwheat), black pepper, salt, and sage. Pour into molds and let cool into lovely brown gelatinous bricks.

To prepare scrapple, slice thinly. Heat a skillet with a little butter or lard until quite hot. Dredge scrapple slices in flour and throw on skillet. Turn down to medium and cook longer than you think you should. Turn once only, and cook the other side. It should be crispy brown. Eat for breakfast with eggs, or do as the Pennsylvania Amish do and make yourself a scrapple sandwich!

In my zeal and my spring delirium, I thought "lovely brown gelatinous bricks" sounded appetizing, which tells you why Mark is in charge of sales.

We were learning, slowly, but everything needed to be done quickly. There was one moment of triumph during potato-planting week. The potatoes—a thousand pounds of them—had already been cut into golf ball–size hunks. Each hunk had at least one eye on it, where the white sprouts were already beginning to emerge. It was a Friday, and we'd spent the morning and noontime harvesting more nettles, moving milk to the distribution refrigerator, making cuts of beef. In the afternoon, while I finished arranging the share for the members, Mark hitched the horses to the cultivator, with one large spade attached straight down the middle. He used it to dig the trenches, taking care to dig them straight, perfectly parallel, forty inches apart. If he wiggled, cultivation and hilling later in the season would be impossible, at least without digging up the very potatoes we were planting. Mark was good at straight lines from the beginning, which I took as a sign of his upright character.

As evening settled in, I took the team from him and put them up in their stalls, still harnessed, then ran back to the field to help him drop the cut potatoes into their trenches, ten inches apart. Before we were finished, the sun had set, and the potatoes still had to be covered. There was a stretch of rain predicted to begin the next day, and we were close to the end of the window for potato planting. Tired as we were, if we wanted potatoes for the year, it had to be done.

Mark kept dropping potatoes, speeding along the rows at a run, while I went back to the barn. Following his hurried instructions, I wrenched the spade off the cultivator and replaced it with a pair of discs, set on an inward-facing V, to push the loose soil over the potatoes in their trench. Then I went to the barn for the dozing horses and rehitched them. Like us, they had already worked overtime that day, and they were probably expecting I'd turn them out on pasture for the night. I hated to ask them to work again, but we didn't have much choice. I was starting to distrust anthropomorphic feelings by then—I suspected that to assign human emotion to animals was to underestimate the beasts—but Sam certainly moved with a sense of purpose that night, leaning into the bit and picking up his feet on the way to the field, practically dragging sluggish old Silver with him.

I had never used the cultivator before, but Mark was the faster potato dropper, so I drew the job of teamster. The wheels and the discs adjust by foot pedal, so the trick is to try to watch where the horses are going and watch the ground underneath your seat, both at the same time. You must keep the row centered perfectly between the horses so that the naked potatoes get buried completely. I found that I was not so good at straight lines and wondered what that meant about *my* character.

Sam, though, was the teacher's pet in our little class of two, and either he had cultivated row crops before or he was a very fast learner. At the end of a row, I'd whoa the team to disengage the heavy discs, and Sam would flick one ear back, listening for the cue to turn. In the pasture, Silver was the undisputed king, but in harness, when he knew the answers, Sam was not afraid to assert himself. He nudged Silver through the turns, sometimes laying his ears back and throwing his weight into it, with attitude.

The moon rose, but it was no help—a pale splinter flanked by the fat spring Venus. By the time we were three-quarters finished, it was truly dark. Mark was still sprinting along the final trenches, dropping potatoes. I couldn't see where the rows started anymore. I was about to yell to Mark that we had to quit and go in when I realized Sam knew exactly what we were doing and could see better than I could in the dark. Soon as we rounded a turn, I'd give him a loose line and he'd find the right place at the top of the row and stop. Silver kerthumped along next to him. When I asked them to step up, the potatoes were right where they were supposed to be, passing between my feet, vague white orbs in deep shadow, and I had nothing to do with it. We finished the whole field that way, the horses' backs steaming in the chilly night air. To this day I don't know why they work for us so willingly. They are big enough to say no, but they keep saying yes, even at the end of a long day, even in the dark.

Part Four
Summer

The first hot days came, and with them the flies. Great green-headed ones that tormented the horses, and the blackflies and deerflies that tormented us; the face flies that gathered at the corners of the cows' eyes, and the carrion flies that lurked everywhere, waiting for spilled blood. We slaughtered the cow we'd named Kathleen first thing after chores, before the flies would be too thick. We'd had the beef cattle checked for pregnancy, and Kathleen was not bred, despite the bull's best efforts. Dr. Goldwasser could feel something wrong with her ovaries, so we'd marked her for culling. She was an interesting-looking cow, dark brown with a beautiful streak of white in her shaggy forelock that made me think of Susan Sontag.

Mark and I moved through the steps of slaughter gracefully now, a coordinated team of two. She was grazing quietly. Mark shot her, in the x between her eyes and ears, and she dropped. Cattle fall with a kind of preordained momentum that seems faster and more forceful somehow than mere gravity. Sheep, too. Chickens, by contrast, flap their way to death, wildly, nervously. Pigs do not go gently but with furious motion. I used to wonder if the differences in those last moments had something to do with the essence of their natures coming out—the pushy pig, the docile cow, the twitchy hen—but now I think they are just tricks of anatomy, the thickness of the skull or the map of nerves.

Mark handed me the gun, I handed him the knife. He cut her throat quickly, and the hot blood poured out on the grass. She bled and kicked, parody of flight, her eyes blank, beyond unconscious. When her reflexive movements slowed, I wrapped a chain around one of her hind legs, and then she kicked again, slowly but purposefully, as though the leg knew what I was doing and was making a final protest, even if it wasn't connected to a brain anymore. I held the leg for a moment, felt the strength seep from the big muscles. It takes time to drain all the life from a living thing, as though life were a substance, some sluggish liquid more viscous than blood, or the sand in the Wicked Witch's hourglass.

You can't watch another creature's death without contemplating your own. I wondered out loud to Mark about the sensations of it. Do you think she felt pain? Do you think she suffered? He said he did not think she felt fear. And he wasn't sure I was asking the right question. The passage out is only a tiny part of the whole. As for himself, compared to the big and endless nothing, he said, he would rather feel something, anything. I told him that if I die while we are together I want him to compost me. "And I hope something eats my heart and my liver," I said. After I've eaten so many other creatures' hearts and livers, it's the least I can do. We were working in a field close to the road, and a couple was approaching, on a prebreakfast power walk. She was wearing a bright blue jog bra and tight black pants, which marked them as summer visitors, city people. We hoisted the carcass up by one leg on the bucket of the tractor. The half-severed head dangled loosely in the air. They looked our way, first with curiosity, then with horror. "You better put that in writing," Mark said.

I'd become familiar enough with the insides of animals by then to have left behind more or less completely the usual squeamishness toward eating parts other than the most common cuts of muscle. One person's scrap is another person's delicacy. At first, Mark and I ate more than our share of the unusual parts, because they weren't very popular then with the members. Things have changed now, and we're lucky if we can get our hands on a piece of liver, but back then our kitchen was a culinary playground. Mark tested and cooked and tested and cooked until he had a stupendous deviled kidney pie, spiked with cream and bacon. My own specialty was heart, the rich, meaty symbol of love. On busy days during the growing season I liked to slice it thin and sauté it, then top each plate with a spoonful of pan gravy. In winter, when the pace was a little slower and nobody minded the all-day heat from a slow oven, I stuffed whole hearts with dried herbs and mushrooms and buttered bread crumbs and braised them. I fell in love all over again with liver, experimenting with the various styles of pâté and terrines. I sought out cookbooks that could offer wisdom on these specialties—Jane Grigson's classic *Charcuterie and French Pork Cookery,* so writerly, and so wise on the odd bits and pieces, like trotters and ears. I read Michael Ruhlman and Brian Polcyn's *Charcuterie,* dry and precise and insistent on the details, which made me feel like a chemist. And then I discovered my enduring favorite, Hugh Fearnley-Whittingstall's *The River Cottage Meat Book,* a book that made nose-to-tail cooking seem accessible, even fun.

Hugh was the one I turned to the first time we slaughtered a bull and the testicles appeared in the refrigerator, the size of oblong softballs, squishy to the touch, covered in a whitish skin marked with squiggly purple blood vessels. "They do not appear very appetizing in the raw," Hugh said reassuringly, "but once prepared, they lose their fearsome aspect and, like brains, I think most people would find them quite palatable if they didn't know what they were." Following Hugh's directions, I blanched them in boiling water for two minutes, skinned them, and marinated them in olive oil, vinegar, green onion, and herbs. I hit a snag on the skinning step, because I couldn't tell what was considered skin on a testicle and what was, well, *other.* I peeled off a layer of membrane only to find another layer. Maybe a testicle is like an onion, I thought, and if I keep peeling, I'll end up with nothing. So I left some of the white and squiggly purple stuff on until I got to slicing them into rounds and discovered that the true interior of a testicle is light brown in color, with a fine granular texture—more prairie uni than prairie oyster, if you ask me. I tossed the slices in seasoned flour and panfried them in butter, and served them for breakfast along with scrambled eggs and toast. The taste was interesting, not too far from a very fresh sea scallop, which the slices resembled in shape and size. I liked them, and Mark loved them. "In Spain," Hugh says, "bull's testicles are considered a great delicacy and an enhancer of masculinity." I wrote him a fan note.

And then there was blood. Solid parts were one thing. Fluids, I wasn't so sure I could handle. They were a kind of last frontier. I checked for Hugh's opinion and found his recipe for black pudding, which he called "the best possible affirmation of your intention to make good use of every last bit of your pig."

I took a pot to the field with me when Mark and I went to slaughter a pig and caught about half a gallon of blood. Following the recipe, I stirred it while it was warm, scooping out the stringy bits that clotted around my spoon. The liquid that remained was intensely red, redder than anything that I'd ever called food before. I sautéed an onion, added sherry, cream, herbs, bread crumbs, and diced pork fat, and mixed all of it into the blood. Mark held the knotted casing for me while I funneled the mixture in. Now I had a set of long red water balloons, still not food. I put a shallow pan on the stove at a gentle simmer and laid the balloons in to poach. Some of them exploded, but the ones that remained intact quickly turned from squishy to firm, and from red to lavender. They looked theoretically edible. Cooled, they were sliceable, dotted with white, succulent bits of fat. They were very rich and asked to be eaten in small bites, but there was nothing challenging about the taste, which was subtle enough to leave room for the sherry and the herbs. The texture was delicate and appealingly mousselike.

Summer advanced, and the fields began to send forth vegetables by the bushel. On Friday mornings, Mark and I got out of bed in the cool dark to harvest bushels of lettuce, spinach, chard, arugula, and snap peas, then baby beets, baby carrots, shell peas. I had never eaten shell peas straight from the field before, and I could not get enough of their sweet green crunch. Thomas LaFountain introduced me to the North Country way of cooking them. Gently simmer freshly shelled peas in milk until they turn bright but not mushy; add salt and pepper and a little butter, and, at the end, a sprig or two of mint. A bowl of spring peas cooked in milk is worth any amount of time spent weeding and picking.

We dug the first new potatoes, the size of eggs, with bright, thin reddish-pink skins. For a week's worth of lunches, Mark and I feasted on boiled new potatoes with butter and salt, and enormous bowls of fresh greens. Eating on the stone bench in front of the house, looking out over our fields, I could see that the farm was beginning to come together. The buildings were still leaning, the farmhouse's window was still broken, but it had a visible sense of purpose now, an animating spark. *It has regained its soul,* I thought.

The members, who had been happy enough with meat, milk, and nettles, were ecstatic when they began getting vegetables. Word of our farm spread, and as the summer went on, our membership doubled, then tripled.

*   *   *

My existence, from daybreak to dark, became focused on the assassination of weeds. Before that first year, I'd filed "agriculture," in the card catalog of my head, in the same general place as "nature." As in many things, I was so wrong. Farming, I discovered, is a great and ongoing war. The farmers are continually fighting to keep nature behind the hedgerow, and nature is continually fighting to overtake the field. Inside the ramparts are the *sativas,* the cultivated plants, soft and vulnerable, too highbred and civilized for fighting. Aligned with nature, there are the weeds, tough foot soldiers, evolved for battle. As we approached the solstice, both sides were at full tilt, stoked by rain and the abundance of sun. Every morning, Mark and I would look out over the fields at first light and see a fresh haze of green. For every one of ours, there were a hundred, a thousand, ten thousand of theirs, wave after wave, unending.

If you ever wonder why organic vegetables cost more, blame weeds. The work on a conventional farm that can be done with one pass of the sprayer must, on an organic farm, be done continually, from germination to harvest, by physically disrupting the weeds. When they have just emerged from the ground—the infant stage called white thread, for the appearance of the first thin taproot—they are easy to kill by barely nudging them, exposing that delicate root to the drying air or burying the new leaves so that they are starved of sun. If allowed to become bigger—the taproot expanding out into a fine white web, the leaves unfolding on a thickening stem—they require increasingly more effort to kill. Much beyond white thread, our tool of choice is a hoe. If the weeds are allowed to grow bigger still, the hoe becomes useless, and the row must be hand-weeded.

Lucky for us, all farmers were once what we now call organic, and the horse-drawn tools they invented to deal with weeds were precise and efficient. The best one in our arsenal was the ancient, rusty International two-horse cultivator we'd bought at the Amish auction. Mark cut a new tongue for it out of green ash and replaced some of its broken parts. Like so many other things that year, it wasn't exactly right—the bearings were bad, so the wheels tilted and flopped on hills and turns—but it was usable. It looked like the two-wheeled sulkies that harness racers drive, but with lots of levers and adjusters and gears stuck on it. It was the kind of machine Willy Wonka would have used if he were a dirt farmer instead of a chocolatier.

I became one with that beautiful tool. I climbed aboard as soon as chores could be finished, the horses brushed and fed and harnessed. The sun would be up by then, the dew burning off. In the field, I adjusted the many levers, which controlled the depth and angle of the sweeps that ran along the ground. The goal was to disrupt the soil as close as possible to the plants without actually killing them. The horses walked on either side of the row, and I rode above it, moving the sweeps from side to side with my feet. It was magic at white thread stage, killing hundreds of thousands of tiny wild mustards and lamb's-quarters on every pass of the field. It was enormously satisfying to finish a row and look back at all the little upended weeds, wilting in the drying air.

From that perspective, I got to know our enemies, and their various strengths and weaknesses. There was crafty smartweed, the plotting intellectual; purslane, the Trojan horse, who rode into the fields on our tools and grew into a formidable foe. There was thistle, the big brute with the mace, slow and obvious but heavily armored, and his timing was pure genius, going to seed at the climax of the season, when we were too busy on other fronts and watched helplessly as the purple blooms changed to white fluff and spread in the wind. Finally there was the pretty, strangling bindweed, a cousin to morning glory, nature's Mata Hari. She was my nemesis.

Bindweed appeared innocuous enough at first. Pale, succulent, vulnerable-looking tentacles that soon produced small heart-shaped leaves. It grew slowly and then seemed to explode, adding inches of vine per day and twining over the young crops, intending to smother. It was largely immune to the sweeps of the cultivator, which were so effective at killing the young annual weeds. Bindweed could not be killed by uprooting or by burying. Some of the weed would tangle in the sweeps and be torn out of the ground, and if it had reached a crop plant, the crop plant would be torn out, too. Then the crop plant would wither and die in the sun, while the bindweed drew on its own moist flesh, rerooted, and grew. As the bindweed gained on us, the vines became luxuriant mats over the ground, and they wrapped around the working parts of the cultivator in the first feet of a row, which turned the sweeps into useless things that dug rough trenches in the ground and made the horses sweat with effort. The only thing to do for bindweed was crawl along the row with a bucket and tear every piece out by hand, haul it away from the field, and dump it. And spit on it. We could spend a whole day clearing the field we called Small Joy, and by the end of it, a new wave of succulent tips was pushing up to the surface of the soil.

Haymaking began. All ears were tuned to the weather radio, all eyes on the grass. We'd hired the Owens family to make our hay that year, old Mr. Owens and his grown sons, Neal and Donald. We could hear familial bickering coming from the machine shop in the evenings as the men worked on the baler. It had a bad knotting mechanism that had confounded the best mechanics in the neighborhood.

We needed five thousand bales of hay to bring our animals through the winter. The success of haying depends on the weather. You have to have a stretch of dry days, so that the grass can be mowed, dried, fluffed, dried some more, then raked into windrows and baled. If hay is rained on, its quality deteriorates. If hay is put into a loft when it is too wet, it heats up and molds. In the worst-case scenario, it heats and heats until it spontaneously combusts and the barn burns down.

During stretches of good weather, the Owenses rushed to make as much hay as possible, and Mark and I left whatever else we were doing to help. I had to learn to drive the tractor, a skill I'd managed to avoid acquiring until then. I didn't hate it as much as I feared it. I was paranoid that my foot would slip off the clutch and I'd run someone down with those unforgiving tires. But haying season is no time to indulge fears. At the end of the day, I climbed up into the cab of the giant orange Same, an Italian machine with enough horsepower to flatten cities, and I drove while the men stacked bales onto the wagon behind me. Once I got used to it, it felt sickly good, like holding a gun. Neal, the largest of the Owenses, could pick up a fifty-pound bale by its strings with his thick fingers and fling it in a graceful arc to its place on the wagon. He made the action look effortless, even delicate, like a girl tossing rose petals. The afternoon light turned the fields golden, and everyone's skin looked tawny.

Sometimes, haymaking continued late into the night. The Owenses brought the bales in from the field, and Mark and I stacked them in the mow. One night I was in the loft alone. There was a big moon, and the sky was clear, but in the mow, it was deeply dark, the single bulb sending its light out in a paltry circle through the dust. Mark was outside, sending the mountain of bales one by one up the hay elevator and through the window. I listened for them to thump to the loft floor, then hauled and heaved them into place. The loft was half full, and the loose bits of hay had been falling all evening under the elevator, and all noise was muted, as in a heavy snow. Suddenly, close to me, I heard a loud panting and rustling and scrabbling sound. My tired mind raced. *"BEAR!"* I shrieked, in the voice I use only for emergencies. It carried through the muted, dusty air of the loft and out the mow and over the clanky elevator to Mark, who shut down the elevator. Then I heard a soft, deep *huh huh huh*. It was Neal, who had hefted himself up the loft ladder with much effort to help me stack the bales, laughing in the dark.

This story had legs. For weeks, when people came by the farm, they'd droll through the open truck window, "I hear you thought ol' Neal was a bear," as though reciting the price of milk.

*   *   *

The peak of summer was the crazy race that Mark had warned me about, a frantic contest of urgency. Haymaking! Fences! Harvest! Weeds! We sprinted through the late plantings of fall carrots and beets. We abused the young cabbage transplants, trotting along a row with a tray of them, throwing them to the ground, then crawling on our knees and slamming each into the dirt with one unnurturing gesture, moving on to the next. The days started at 3:45 A.M. Chores before dawn, out in the fields with the horses by the time the sun was fully up, then work, work, work, racing the weather, the weeds, the season. One afternoon, I fell asleep on the cultivator at the end of a row and dreamed I was on a boat. Evening milking started at 4:30 P.M., and cleanup and chores were over by 7:00, but the chickens would not roost until 9:00 and had to be closed into their coop so they wouldn't be eaten by owls. Too few hours later, the whole thing began again.

Mark seemed to have tapped into a secret and possibly diabolical source of energy. I'd never seen him so exuberant, so excessively cheerful. He sang in Spanish while he washed dishes or picked peas. When we worked in the field together, he took new interest in subjects he'd known nothing about, asking me about pop culture and the romantic lives of stars he would not have recognized if they'd walked out onto our field and bonked him on the head with a hoe. He questioned me closely on what exactly a hipster was, and whether or not I had been one when we'd met. Those weeks were intensely happy ones for me, too. In my weekly note to the members, I enthused, "Did you *see* the sunrises this week?" and "The zinnias in the Home Field are frankly rioting."

In the evenings, we'd walk the fields again, to see how our new seeds had germinated, which sections were most in need of weeding. We made lists, ranked according to urgency. The striped cucumber beetles had descended thickly on the cucurbits in Mailbox Field and eaten the newly transplanted buttercup squashes to lace. Walking downwind of them one evening, we could smell them, an acrid stinkbug stink, like nail polish remover and armpit. They moved to the top of the list, and the next morning, while the bugs were still torpid and flightless, we walked through the field, knocked them into buckets of soapy water, and crushed big heaps of them under our heels on the driveway.

Farmers toil. Nature laughs. Farmers weep. There's your history of agriculture in a nutshell. At the climax of the season, when we needed him most desperately, Silver got hurt. I noticed it in the morning, with the team harnessed, walking down the driveway on the way to the spring-tine harrow. His big head jerked up a little too high each time his left front hoof touched the ground and bobbed a little too low when he stepped down on the right side. I drove them back to the barn, left Sam in his stall, and took Silver back out to the hard-packed dirt driveway. Holding him by the bridle, I coaxed him into a trot, running alongside him just to be sure. At that point, the lameness showed up as a subtle disturbance of rhythm. By afternoon, when Dr. Goldwasser came, poor Silver was gimping around like a wounded soldier, barely able to touch the foot to the ground. He had a puncture in his sole, a deep, inch-long cut. I'd driven him through the barnyard, near where we'd pulled down one of the old buildings, and it had probably happened there—an old nail or a piece of sharp metal or a badly angled hunk of glass. At least he hadn't injured the flexor tendon inside his hoof. He would probably be fine. But he needed rest, a course of antibiotics, bandages, and daily soaks in a bucket of hot water and Epsom salts. The soaking and the dressing were highly exhausting, because he took great joy in stepping on the bucket instead of in it, and when he decided he'd had enough fooling, he planted his big foot and flatly refused to pick it up. And the rest? If he were a saddle horse, forced rest would have been an annoyance. Because he was half our source of traction at the busiest point in the season, it was a catastrophe.

All we could do was keep trying. We were making it up as we went along. I remember feeling a kind of reverse nostalgia then, a longing for the future, when the canon would be established, when we would know what to expect and be equipped to handle it.

The heat came down on us like a solid thing, as though to make up for the frigid winter. The pace of growth redoubled. In the North Country, the plants have to seize the day. You could practically hear them growing; I imagined the cells dividing and madly redividing with tiny pops, the pace of their metabolism stoked by the abundance of light, heat, and rain.

The quack grass sent forth its spidery shoots, threatening

to strangle the new carrots, the young beets. We pulled the one-horse cultivator out of the back of the pole barn. Next to the two-horse cultivator, it was a blunt and puny tool, a simple adjustable V that runs between the rows, teeth on the bottom, a clevis for the horse at the pointy end and handles for the humans behind. Like the plow, it's meant to be a one-person operation, the lines buckled behind the shoulders, hands guiding the handles. I hooked Sam to it and gave it my best shot, but on the first pass I killed more carrots than weeds. Mark tried, with the same result. In times of crisis, you fall back on what you know. I unbuckled the long lines from Sam's bridle, Mark helped me vault onto his back, and I rode him, using the strap of his checkline for reins. Mark walked behind, guiding the cultivator. It cost us two passes for every row against the two-horse cultivator's one, and it took two people, quadruple the work, but it was good at uprooting the quack. I must have looked small way up there on Sam's back. A neighbor stopped by the house to ask who the child was, riding the cultivating horse. "That was my job when *I* was a child," he said.

Without Silver, the tide of the war turned against us. Rains came at bad times, keeping us out of the field, throwing the advantage to the weeds. Whole sections of fields were lost when they grew way beyond white thread stage and would need to be hand-pulled. We walked the fields in the rain for an emergency triage, decided to sacrifice the young parsnips and the last planting of cabbage. They were overrun and would have required too much time to save, and the weeds were not far from setting seed. A single amaranth can produce two hundred thousand seeds, which can wait in the soil for decades for the opportunity to sprout. If we let them go, we'd be sowing our own future problems. When the rain stopped I harrowed those rows into the ground, weeds and our plants meeting the same end, and afterward I felt the relief that a traitor feels when the dirty work is done.

Our friends and neighbors helped. They saved us. Mike and Laurie Davis came over with all three of their sons and spent a whole Saturday hand-weeding the onions with us at a time when their own farm's needs were just as urgent. Lars came to see what we were up to on his land and was immediately pressed into service, clearing the last bits of old wheat and dead rats from the granary so we could use it to store new grain. He returned almost weekly throughout the season for more, launching into whatever job was most urgent with his characteristic enthusiasm. Mark's best friend, Matt, came from his farm in New Jersey, bringing his young son, Jack. Matt and Mark had worked together at Genesis, a biodynamic vegetable farm founded by radical nuns. It was humbling to watch them harvest, each of them stripping two double rows of peas in the time it took me to work my way down one. While I dunked the peas in cold water to take the heat of the field out of them, Matt helped Mark slaughter a steer. (I worried it would upset Jack, who was six, but he was used to the sight of a big animal's insides. "Feels like a basketball," he said mildly, poking the steer's taut and enormous first stomach.) Mark's sister Linda Brook had run her own farm before her first child was born, and she and her family came to visit and were promptly put into the potatoes, hauling out the tall yellow wild mustard plants that were threatening to drop their seed. My father drove up for two- and three-day stretches and took over Mark's job, steering the one-horse cultivator while I rode Sam. He still talks about how heartbroken he was then to see us work so hard for something that was so clearly doomed to fail. One afternoon a carload of young tourists from Maine stopped to take pictures of the horse and the cultivator. Mark met them in the field, talking fast, and before they knew what was happening, he'd pressed hoes into their hands and put them to work in the carrots.

On our evening farm walks, the list of crops to harvest grew longer. We cruised the peas as the sun went down, grazing on handfuls of pods so full they looked dented. Next to them, the deer had gotten into the lettuces, taking a bite from the very heart of each head, sampling a hundred but eating none to the end. Mark liked to graze lettuces that way in the evening, too. He'd cut a head from its base with his knife and sink his face into it, ripping the sweet center with his teeth, casting away the rest. This is the farmer's privilege, a form of decadence, and it made us feel rich.

Question: Why is farming like a relationship?
Answer: Because you do not reap what you sow. That's a lie. You reap what you sow, hill, cultivate, fertilize, harvest, and store.

Silver healed. A hailstorm missed us. The worst of the crisis passed. The tomatoes were heavy on the vine. The corn neared the cusp of its glory, doing its brave best, ten feet tall in the good places. Corn! That's what it said when I looked at it, the exclamation point green as its leaves in my mind. The onions had collapsed at the neck, laying their leaves on the ground. "What's wrong with them?" I asked Mark. "Nothing," he said. "It's senescence. They've finished growing."

The grass that had been left to its own devices was up to my chest. When we walked the mowed margins of the fields in the evenings, a school of black crickets sprang ahead of us like dolphins in front of a ship. The pond behind the farmhouse had shrunk to half its size, and it was thick with frogs. Every afternoon, the great blue heron came, patience in the form of a bird. Still, still, and then a movement too quick to be seen. The heron had gigged a frog. The frog struggled at the end of the heron's bill, and the heron tilted his wedge of a head to the sky, swallowed, and resumed his perfect stillness, one skinny chorus-girl leg cocked backward at the knee.

Some new weather settled in, heavy with humidity, and the farm felt almost oppressively fertile. The zucchini grew monstrous overnight, flies blanketed a knuckle bone left in the hot grass with their eggs. Just a tick past fruition sits decay.

The spokesthing for the hot decline of the season was the tomato hornworm. Who knew these creatures existed? Fat as Mark's thumb and at least as long, they had smooth, soft skin the color of a Granny Smith apple, with white filigree details. Looked at one way, they were beautiful, meticulously crafted pieces of living art; another way, and they were horrible, soft, voracious aliens. Either way, I had to admire the camouflage, which was so good I could stare at a damaged plant for ages before I saw the worm, though the evidence of its presence was obvious: leaves missing, whole stems consumed, big, wet clumps of black frass. Sometimes, when I was close but still couldn't see it, the worm gave itself up with a faint but menacing clickclickclickclick. Mark had told me they bite, so I plucked each one off with my Leatherman and rubbed it into the dirt with my boot. The insides were a bright green jelly; the seven-chambered heart continued to pulse in the dust. I did not dare turn my back on it until it was still.

July hustled by, and the crops edged closer to assured. By August, the wall of frost was coming, so new weeds were less worrisome. Frost would kill them for us before they set seed. We stayed up half the night to get the wedding invitations out, and once they slid through the slot at the post office, I felt a terrible dread.

This man I was supposed to be marrying, he was maddening. I was maddening with him. We generated a ferocious energy together. I remember in my early twenties talking with my sister, ten years my senior, about the nature of marriage. She was just out of one then, and wise. There are two kinds, she said. The comfortable kind and the fiery kind. Mark and I, we were tinder, just begging for a spark.

The things I admired most about him in the abstract were what drove me nuts in the specific. He was a believer. When he was fifteen, he was home alone after school one day when the Jehovah's Witnesses knocked on the door. He opened it and invited them in. When his parents came home, many hours later, they found him giving an exegesis on his personal credo, which he had typed into a five-page document. The Witnesses were silent on the other end of the couch.

By the time I met him, his credo had been informed by his studies and a lot of travel in the developing world. He'd spent time in villages and cities in Kenya, Ecuador, and Mexico with his family, then, after college, he'd lived and worked for stretches in Venezuela and India. To him, the impoverished lives, loss of rural culture, and environmental degradation in those places seemed tied to the world's accelerating cycle of production and consumption. He saw that cheap goods cost somebody, somewhere, plenty, but by the time they reached the big-box shelves thousands of miles away, those costs were invisible. He became uncomfortable with processes he could not see, impacts he could not measure.

These were not extraordinary conclusions, and many other people all over the world have seen and acknowledged them, and then gone on living more or less the same way they have all along. Mark was not one of those people. He tried, as much as possible, to live outside of the river of consumption that is normal life in America. He preferred secondhand everything, from underwear to appliances. Even better than secondhand was handmade. He dreamed aloud to me of someday making his own toothbrushes out of boars' bristles. He hated plastic, couldn't stand the thought of adding more of it to the world. He hated waste. When we met he owned a big ball of his own used dental floss, which he was keeping, he said vaguely, because it was useful. When pressed for specifics, he said he might need it one day to stitch up a rip in his pants.

He thought about the effects of every quotidian decision. Once, when we were living in New Paltz, we had a discussion on the way to the store about whether it was better to buy organic food that was not local or local food that was not organic. It was a one-sided discussion, a monologue really, and it was long, because my old Honda had finally died, and he'd resisted replacing it, and for a brief while I'd played along, so we were riding to the store on the red tandem bicycle left over from his last relationship. When we got to the store I picked up a jar of some bitter coffee substitute that I wanted to try, to attempt to methadone myself off of the absurd amount of coffee I was drinking at the time, and he pointed out that it was neither local *nor* organic and suggested I put it back. I found that shocking and ridiculous and bought it anyway.

My friends and I, we weren't big believers. We pretty much closed out the age of irony. If we believed in anything, it was in the coolness of the Lower East Side Mexican place that would sell you illegal margaritas in to-go cups. For me, rules were kind of like accessories, nice things to have but detachable. But what is your ethic? Mark would ask, when we got entangled in a disagreement about the right way to do something on the farm. I don't *have* an ethic, I'd say. I'm from New York. I'm a hedonist.

His beliefs were not all grim and pious. They had a lot of leavening. He believed in the basic goodness and generosity of the world and its people. The world, in general, responded to him with goodness and generosity. When it didn't, he largely ignored it, and was undeterred. My own belief in the goodness and generosity of the world was contingent on constant positive feedback, which I suppose made it less a belief than a hypothesis.

All this believing gave Mark an unbending strength. Without it, we never would have gotten through our first season. We never would have learned, through all the difficulties, how to farm with horses. It was what allowed him to convince other people to get onboard with us. To a person like me, untethered from the values I grew up with and not firmly in possession of my own, this was terribly attractive. But in those weeks before the wedding, I was keenly aware that unbending strength is almost exactly the same as rigidity, and that Mark could be blinkered by it, and unforgiving of people like me, who were neither as sure nor as tenacious as he.

And that stubborn courage, sometimes it made him a daredevil, sometimes it slipped into foolish. A few years after we started, we hired employees, and Mark sent two of them, James and Paige, to the fifty-acre field where the beef herd had wintered, to castrate a new calf. They came back looking pale, the calf still in possession of his testicles. The mother cow, they reported, had gotten agitated when James grabbed her baby's leg, and they'd decided that the job would be safer with three people. "Oh, bah," Mark said. He'd castrated plenty of calves all by himself, with the mama bawling and shaking her head at him. You just have to be quick and decisive and not look so scared, he advised. James and Paige had worked with us long enough by then not to give in to their boss. "*You* do it, then," James said.

The mother in question was named Sinestra, a young black cow with a blunted left horn. She'd lost her first calf the year before, during a stretch of cold, wet weather. Mark and I had spotted him way out in the field, with Sinestra standing over him, mooing pitifully. In the early days I used to see a sleeping creature from a distance in the field and worry, unreasonably, that it was dead, and I'd make a lot of noise until I startled it into getting up. But dead things are too flat and still, and there is some other subtle thing that you can see, maybe the absence of suppleness. Once you've seen it, death is obvious, even from a distance, and that calf was very, very dead, a little heap of wet brown leaves.

Sinestra, though, didn't understand. All she knew was that her bag was aching and her baby wouldn't move. When we got closer, we could see how much she'd been licking him, because his fur was all in tufts. We'd come to the field to feed the herd their hay, and once the wagon was empty, we drove out to pick up the carcass, which would otherwise encourage scavenging, which can lead to predation. We loaded the calf on the wagon and took him away, but Sinestra lingered around that spot in the field for days, searching, lowing. I think that in her wordless way she blamed us for her loss, and I think that's what was in her head when she saw Mark coming across the field with the elastrator, aiming for her boy.

The way it usually goes, the hardest part of castrating a bull calf is catching him. They are fast almost from birth, and they can duck and spin, but if you get to one before he's a week old, it's not impossible; a good sprint or two and you've got him. After that, you just flip him on his back, feel to make sure both testicles are present and accounted for, and use the four-pronged elastrator to slip a tight, heavy rubber band around their base. Then you let him go. The mother cow usually hovers nearby giving you the hairy eyeball, but it's all over so fast, she doesn't have time to organize her molasseslike thoughts into action.

Sinestra, though, must have been thinking ahead. I was not there to see it, but James and Paige were. Mark had taken them along to show them how it is done. As soon as Mark touched the calf, they said, Sinestra charged. Mark was not convinced she was serious, so he kept working, and Sinestra knocked him flat and then tried to rub him into the ground with her big horns. James and Paige had been watching from a safe distance, but when it got serious they ran in, arms flapping, and hazed her away. Sinestra, the little black calf in tow, lit out for the metal barn with no sides, where the rest of the herd was calmly eating hay.

At this point, most people would count themselves lucky to have gotten through such an experience without serious injury and gone home to figure out a new way. Mark, being Mark, dusted himself off and decided to have one more go. This time, he hadn't even gotten hold of the calf before Sinestra charged him. She'd worked out the kinks in her plan on the first charge. This time, it was business. Mark darted for cover behind one of the barn's metal I-beams, and Sinestra ran squarely into it, with spectacular force, so that the whole barn shook. It was only then that Mark decided her son could keep his testicles for the time being.

There is a little coda to this story, though, and, to be fair to Mark and his dang magic circle, I have to tell it. A few days after the Sinestra incident, while we were all still having a good laugh about it at Mark's expense, we got a call from a couple looking specifically for a black Highland bull calf to raise as their herd sire. Black is relatively rare in the breed, and Sinestra's boy was the only black one in our herd. They were willing to pay a premium, so that black calf and his untouched testicles were sold at a tidy profit.

The wedding was to happen on the farm, and all these people from my past would be arriving to see my new life. My parents' many friends were all invited. These people from my hometown had sent me off into the world with great hopes for my future. I'd been given the enormous gift of an Ivy League education and had moved on from there to the gleaming, mysterious city, and now this. I felt that they had certain expectations of me, that they had a right to them, and that those expectations would probably be dashed by the sight of a scurrying rat or the smell of pig manure. I had a lot of anxiety about the wedding.

We chose the site for our ceremony, a rolling thirty-acre field in the middle of the farm, a little higher than the surrounding land. It was one of our best fields, well-drained and full of clover. We'd grazed it, rested it, and then cut the hay from it late in the season, so that as summer waned and fall came on, it looked like acres and acres of perfectly manicured lawn. The hedgerow on three sides was old and full of large trees and stretches of stone fence, elegant signifiers of another farmer's work. On the fourth side the hedgerow was young and the trees were mostly brush and saplings, except for one twisty, old oak that stood in the middle, towering over everything. No film scout could find a location that said bucolic wedding more sweetly, and the oak—sturdy, ancient thing—seemed an auspicious symbol of permanence and stability. It was a half-mile walk from the barnyard, too far for some of our guests, so we planned to shuttle them down with the horses and a long green wagon with bench seats that we borrowed from Shane Sharpe. We would have the reception dinner and a dance in the loft of the west barn. That would require some work, since the barn was empty of hay but full of pigeons, had no lights, and could be reached only by means of a ladder up the side.

I tried to see our house the way our guests would see it. It had its good points. It was square and solid, sturdy like a stevedore. The year 1902 was scratched into the foundation, and it had withstood all those winters and summers; Mark's father, who had built houses for a living, said it had been well and carefully constructed. It had large mullioned windows and two chimneys. The old kitchen chimney was made of bricks, and it was in ruins inside. We'd broken into it through the wall above our stove to investigate, and the hole remained, covered by a tinfoil pie plate. The newer chimney, on the east side, was made of mason blocks, ugly but sound.

I had seen old pictures of the farmhouse as it had been designed, and it was beautiful then, with a neat stone walk leading to an open, columned porch, which shaded the front door. By the time we arrived the porch had been clumsily enclosed and the columns hidden, and the roof over the porch had been lowered slightly and angled differently, and the large windows on the second floor had been replaced with small, tight, cheap things that made the house look like it was squinting. One of them was still cracked, as it had been when we arrived. The gracious front door was unused, victim of the dastardly porch renovation. We entered through the slapped-on mudroom, where a leaking roof had made large stained holes in the wallboard and there was a perpetual smell of dampness. Those leaks proved obstinate, resulting from a problem with the way the roof was joined on. The holes in the drywall were still there; we made a stab at decency by squaring the ragged edges so the straggly material wouldn't brush people's heads when they walked through our door.

Inside, the house was a travesty, the good vernacular details—plaster-and-lath walls, hardwood floors—covered over with linoleum, green carpets, peeling paper, plywood paneling (standard-issue brown downstairs; upstairs, white and a green not found in nature), and, in the kitchen, a distressed faux-brick facing that never fooled anyone, even when it was new. Those elements came, as far as we could tell, from the last renovation, done thirty years ago, and since then the house had seen hard use. We'd heard in town that at one point there were sixteen people living in it, all of them just out of high school. They'd left behind fist-size holes punched into the wallboard, NASCAR stickers on the backs of doors, phone numbers scribbled in pencil on the white-and-green paneling.

I had dreams for the house. I believed in its good bones. But in the chaos of the farm's start-up year, I treated it badly—worse even than all the previous tenants, who at least kept the floors swept and vacuumed. The first floor was always muddy from the constant traffic of boots fresh from the field. One afternoon that summer, poor old Nico got locked in the mud-room during a thunderstorm. She was terrified of thunder, and she panicked and tried to dig and bite her way through the room's door. Nico was fine, but the metal door was seriously mangled, bent and ripped at the bottom, and we had not had time to replace it.

In the kitchen, we'd installed an industrial-size, three-bay, stainless-steel sink, and above it we tacked a rude drain rack made of steel pipe and wire mesh, where we stored the milk cans and stainless-steel buckets until we had a milk house. We had screwed a heavy hook into the kitchen ceiling for hanging quarters of beef while butchering until we had a proper butcher shop. They gave the kitchen a rough, industrial, S and M kind of look. There were no curtains on the windows, and our furniture was minimal, hand-me-downs from family mostly, plus a few things salvaged from my apartment in New York. We didn't own a couch, only the hard, unyielding dining room chairs around a big pine table. There is no sitting here, the house said. Only work or sleep.

We were the only people in town who did not keep our lawn neatly mowed. In Essex, even the scofflaws and the drunks, the wife beaters and the serial unemployed mow their lawns. On the outskirts, there might be cars up on blocks in the yard, permanent fixtures, but the grass around them was cut on a weekly basis. Our elderly neighbors, the Everharts, kept their lawn both neatly trimmed and thoroughly decorated, with figurines, birdbaths encircled by pansies, and a kind of weather-proof slide projector set up to make a picture against the house at night, a different image for every holiday, from a flag at the Fourth of July to a snowman at Christmas.

Meanwhile, our lawn grew shaggy. I looked at it as I ran by with my hands full of crates or tools or stakes, feeling a growing self-loathing, knowing that it was a black mark against us in the collective mind of our community, a civic failure. One evening at the beginning of summer I'd grabbed the little electric mower my parents had given us and made an attempt to cut it, but by then the grass had grown so rank it was like trying to shear a sheep with nose hair clippers. I made one crushed, chewed-up stripe of grass at the lawn's periphery and was defeated. By August the lawn was so overgrown it could swallow dogs and small children. Our community has more than its fair share of eccentrics, and it is tolerant of them, but I could tell the lawn bothered our neighbors, because they didn't tease us about it. Others of our quirks—such as the pair of Highland horns that Shane Sharpe helped Mark bolt onto the hood of our Honda, making the car look like it's sporting a handlebar mustache—they would tease us about incessantly. About the lawn, they were ominously silent.

Mark is immune to this kind of social pressure, and generally contemptuous of lawns. In his mind, grass is for grazing. And therein lay the solution. We might never find time to mow the lawn, but if it looked fecund enough, and the cattle were hungry, we could find the time to put up a fence. A few weeks before our wedding, we ringed the lawn with electric fence and moved the beef herd onto it. The dairy herd was recruited for the smaller patch across the driveway.

For three days, the cattle mowed our lawn. We fell asleep to Rupert calling to the dairy cows: a series of mournful, falling bass notes, the sound of a monumental desire. Then a petulant trumpeting, the pitch rising to what passes for tenor in a bull, the sound of desire thwarted by electric fence. We awoke to the gentle rip-rip sound of cows grazing right outside our bedroom window and ate breakfast, on a foggy dawn, to the mamas bellowing through the mist to find their sleepy babies. While brushing my teeth, I watched them from the upstairs bathroom window. They'd disturbed the mallard who was nesting next to the pond, but the tree swallows were thrilled with the boost in fly population. I opened the window and helloed to the cattle, and they answered, in chorus, and raised their heads, jaws working, to look for me. By the time they moved on to fresh pasture, the lawn was a lawn again, nipped neatly to within an inch of the ground. The neighbors nodded their approval, and I checked "mow lawn" off the wedding to-do list.

My friend Alexis came for another visit at the end of summer, on her way to Greece. When we were both college students, she and I had worked as travel writers for a summer on the same assignment in Rome, where we sat outside the Pantheon and ate gelato and watched black-haired boys zip past us on Vespas.

It was the last day of the county fair. Grease gone old in the frying vats, the carnies' cries hoarse now, and weary. The horse trailers and pickups were pulling up to the barns to load the 4-H projects: geese and rabbits and hens, calves, ponies, sheep, plus cots and sleeping bags, coolers, currycombs and hoof polish and electric clippers. The animals looked weary. The kids looked weary. The parents looked weary. In the barn, the teenagers had decorated their horses' stalls with plastic flowers and bunting, photographs, ribbons from the show, sentiments on poster board in felt-tipped cursive ("Thank you,

Lord, for giving us horses and for giving us Jesus, who saves us from hell") and, on one, a memorial, for someone's uncle just killed in Russia, drowned, it said specifically, an accident, in the Black Sea. We emerged from the barn into the bright afternoon. The Ferris wheel turned against a cloudless sky. Next door, in Floral Hall, the antiabortion people had lined the edge of their table with pink plastic fetuses. The Republicans had a table, and I waved to our neighbor Ron, who was handing out red, white, and blue pamphlets there. Across the crowded floor a bearded man was selling tooled leather goods, his stall hung with purses and belts, the buckles of the latter embossed with surprised-looking bucks carrying enormous racks of horn.

Back outside, we passed the duck pond, the pony rides, and the exotic-animal man, who was packing up his snakes. Alexis and I lined up in front of a trailer to buy corn dogs and snow cones. They were advertising a plastic mug of soda the size of a pony keg. I was wondering who in the world would buy such a thing when the three people in line in front of us and the guy behind us each ordered one. The crowd was flowing toward the grandstand, wrists bent under the weight of their kegs of soda, lining up for tickets to the demolition derby. It cost five dollars to get into the grandstand for the derby, on top of the ten dollars at the gate to get into the fair, kids included, so a family of four had dropped sixty dollars before they even bought a hot dog or a gallon of soda, and they were ready to see some action.

In the stands were halter tops and tank tops, tattoos, skinny girls and heavy women, pockets sticking out the bottoms of cutoff shorts. T-shirts with the logos of oil companies, car companies. Many small children were bouncing like pinballs against the patient legs of the extended family.

They'd put up heavy concrete forms to make barriers on the horse-racing track, forming a rectangle about fifty yards long. A tanker from the DOT sprayed water on the dirt surface until it was several inches deep in mud. Outside the barriers the derby cars were lining up. For the last several weeks groups of men had been working on those cars in their backyards, evenings and weekends, a multigenerational tradition, sacred as Christmas. They had souped up the engines and taken the glass out of the windshields, chained closed the doors and trunks, replaced the regulation gas tanks with little one-gallon boxes. Some drivers had lashed foam padding to their doorframes with duct tape. The cars were decorated with checkerboards and stripes, some painted with martial phrases ("It's Gonna Hurt"), some with humor ("I like beer") and some with names of family and loved ones ("Dad + Samantha," "Hi Foxy," and "Jessica Our Angle," that unfortunate misspelling done in careful block letters on a 1980s Olds painted bright green). There were twelve cars per heat. They roared onto the track like motorized lions, like mechanical testosterone, an American bullfight.

The first heat was the four-cylinder, small cars. They lined up in four rows of three, front to back. I asked the family next to us to explain how it worked and they told us that the last car that can still move is the winner, that the experienced drivers ram the others with the backs of their cars, not the fronts, to spare the engines, and they don't do it too hard if they want to finish in the money. Others—the less experienced, or the ones who just can't help themselves—floor their gas pedals and

T-bone their opponents with everything they've got, smashing their own cars in the process.

The green flag waved and the cars screeched toward one another. It was too loud, suddenly, to hear yourself whoop, a wall of general noise. When metal hit metal you didn't hear it as much as feel the impact in your bones. The drivers rocked from side to side inside their cars, helmets bumping off the glassless doorframes. Within seconds there were flames shooting from the hood of one car, and oily smoke drifting up into the stands, and the flagman stopped the action while the firefighters came out with their extinguishers.

The heat lasted ten minutes. It wound down slowly, as cars stalled or got stuck. By the end there was only one car barely moving, and this limping survivor was declared the winner. The track was littered with dead machines, smoke and steam rising from them, leaking fluids. Two four-wheel-drive trucks came onto the track then to tow the losers away. The drivers of the trucks were high school boys—jeans, baseball caps, no shirts to hide their smooth chests—and they exuded proprietary know-how as they maneuvered among the cars. There were pretty girls with long hair and tan shoulders in the front seats next to them and also in the truck beds, which had been tricked out with upholstered seats pushed up next to the cabs. The girls wore spaghetti-strap tanks and short shorts and big hoop earrings and large sunglasses, and did not smile, and pretended that nobody was looking at them.

The bigger cars went next, and then the muscle cars, and later, there would be the moms in minivans division, but by then we couldn't take it anymore. The smoke, the noise, the tension. On top of the roar of the fair, it was all too much, and we were exhausted. The heats would go on for hours, and the winners would be pitted against one another, until the final winner got a thousand-dollar check. Alexis and I stepped over legs and feet and brushed through the riveted crowd, out of the grandstand, back to the row of booths hung with pink beehives of cotton candy, oversize stuffed animals. The lights were coming on now, and under their gaudy glow and into the twilight beyond, pairs of middle school boys and girls walked twined together, fair dates, shouting loudly to each other to belie the intimacy of their touching, as though loudness could render their desire invisible.

Part Five
Fall

The fields are a clock read in colors. As the days of summer passed, the palette of our world shifted from bright greens to dark greens, then ocher, dun, all the variations of gold. The days grew shorter, the light took on a golden cast. Spots of color spread through the trees—reds, oranges, and yellows. The pumpkins became beacons against the dull earth. The late-planted sunflowers bloomed, and their heads, ten feet in the air, were crazy with bees. The goldenrod blossoming in the hedgerow matched exactly the color of the wedding rings I'd kept in a box for more than a year. I'd bought them from a gold merchant in Burma when I was there on an assignment, right after we got engaged. I bought them without knowing Mark's ring size. I guessed his finger was bigger than that of your average Burman, so I'd scoured the market stalls for the biggest ring I could find. I found it and its mate in a shop hung with red silk and smelling of sandalwood. They were twenty-four-karat, dark yellow, simply rounded, heavy, with a dull finish, as deliciously plain and austere as gold can ever be. Mine was too big, and I guessed Mark's would be too small, but I figured I could get them resized at home. When I told the merchant that, she was alarmed. "No cut," she said, tapping the rings with her two fingers. "Bad luck. No break love."

It was September, deep harvest season, days of pulling carrots, pulling beets, stacking hundred-pound bags in the root cellars. Mark scythed the rows of black beans and kidney beans, dry and hard in their brittle pods, and I forked them, stems and all, onto the wagon, which the horses drew slowly down the row. We hauled home a shaky stack that rose six feet above the deck of the wagon, spread them on the concrete floor of the pavilion, and commenced to whack the beans loose with flails we'd made out of pieces of broomstick looped together with baling twine.

When whole sections of the fields had been harvested, we spread them with compost, to replenish the soil with nutrients and get it ready for next year's crops. The compost came from our own pile, which was seven feet tall and twelve feet wide, and snaked sixty feet across the farmyard. The heart of it was made of eleven tons of spoiled field corn that a grain-growing neighbor had given us in the winter, when we'd first arrived. On top of the corn we'd piled layers of all the organic things we had no better use for: manure, weeds pulled from the fields, urine-soaked straw bedding, unwholesome hay, bushels of spent vegetables that didn't appeal to the pigs or the chickens, plus the parts of the animals we butchered that we don't eat: the hide, intestines, stomach, spleen, pancreas, lungs, hooves, horns.

Given the right balance of carbon and nitrogen, the appropriate amount of water, and enough mass, a compost pile can digest anything that was once alive. Throughout the previous winter, delicate clouds of steam had risen from it, like smoke at a disco. It had smelled, not unpleasantly, like a slightly moldy tortilla set on a hot griddle. It was warm enough on top to hatch flies. One foot under the surface, it was hot enough to burn the life out of weed seeds, hot enough to burn your curious hand. Of all the confounding things I encountered that first year, the heat of decomposition—its intensity and duration—was the most surprising, the one that made me want to slap my knee and say, Who knew? That heat comes from the action of hordes of organisms, some so tiny billions can live in a tablespoon of soil. They are in there, eating and multiplying and dying, feeding on and releasing the energy that the larger organisms—the plants and the animals—stored up in *their* time, energy that came, originally, from the sun. I think it's worth it, for wonder's sake, to stick your hand in a compost pile in winter and be burned by a series of suns that last set the summer before.

Throughout the winter and into the spring, we had turned the pile with the tractor's bucket loader, pushing the cool material from the top and edges to the still-hot middle. After mixing, the temperature spiked again, but not as high. Mix, cook, cool, repeat. The volume of the pile shrank and shrank, and by the end of summer, it was reduced by half, its individual components melted into a uniform substance rich in nitrogen, crumbly and black, ready to spread on the fields.

Mark had spent a few late nights in the machine shop that week, rebuilding the horse-drawn manure spreader we'd bought to spread our compost. He and I filled it a quarter of the way full with shovels of our compost and took it to the field to test it out. It was a slick old machine. A wagon, basically, with a narrow, high-sided wooden box. Two chains ran along the bottom of the box, toward a set of three beaters in the back. The chains and the beaters were geared to the wagon's wheels. When I engaged the gears and the horses moved forward, the chain moved and the beaters spun and our compost was flung in a high, wide arc behind the moving wagon. Mark and I cheered. Then, halfway down the row, the beaters kicked a clod of compost forward instead of back. It sailed past my head and whacked Silver on the rump. Startled, he laid his ears back and moved faster. The chain and the beaters moved faster, too, and got louder. The horses, unnerved, tried to run, and it took all my strength to hold them back. After that, Silver seemed to distrust the spreader. When I engaged the gears, his neck tensed and his head shot up high.

The horses and I could spread a ton of compost in the time it took to cross the long edge of our field, which was less than three minutes. The tedious part of the job was loading that ton of compost into the spreader. Mark helped me shovel it in with a pitchfork, by hand, and each load took twenty minutes. As the day wore on, we got tired, and each load took longer still. By afternoon, the tractor, with its bucket loader, began to look very attractive. It could do the same work in two effortless scoops. The only problem was, Silver hated that tractor. When we passed it, parked in the barnyard, he eyed it as though it were a crouching wolf. I worried that the sound of it roaring behind him, in his blind spot, would be too much for him. But we were tired, and it was getting late. Mark fired up the tractor, promising to stop and turn it off if Silver got worked up. I got off my seat on the spreader and went to the horses' heads, because that's what I'd always done with riding horses, to give them confidence.

I remember what happened next as though it were a movie. Wide shot of me at the horses' heads, holding one bridle in each hand, watching Silver's ears. Then a close-up on the blue bucket of the tractor, brimming with compost. The soundtrack is a throbbing diesel engine. Cut to Silver dancing a little but holding it together. Then the bucket dumping into the spreader, Silver going hollow-backed and stiff, the bucket clanking once against the metal side of the spreader, and Silver exploding, his weight on his haunches, his front end off the ground, his head eight feet in the air, my hand no longer on his bridle. Then we see the back ends of two horses at a dead run, the spreader rocketing down the long driveway toward the road, the futile lines between the rolling wheels of the spreader, as impossible to reach as the moon.

I've had more than one opportunity to wonder, since then, what it feels like to be a horse running away. I know there is fear, but also I think there's a certain kind of joy, or if not joy then exhilaration, abandon. The broke horse is always poised between his instincts and his training, and running is giving in to the instinct, the powerful impulse to use his long legs for what they evolved for, to put distance between himself and his death. That's why a horse that has been through a runaway once cannot be fully trusted again. The option of escape has been opened.

I don't remember making the choice to jump clear of Silver when he reared, only that suddenly I was clear, and the horses were running. The noise of the spreader clanging along the driveway was like gas on a fire. Instead of running from the sound of the tractor, the horses were running from the loud, inescapable thing hitched behind them. They ran with their necks stretched out, bits resting loose in their mouths, full gallop. Ridiculously, I ran after them. I remember stripping off my jacket and dropping it on the driveway, as though that could make me run faster. The distance between me and the horses was impossible within seconds, and it opened up, wider and wider. By the time they reached the end of the driveway they were a hundred yards away from me. I tried to will them to stop before they reached the road. They did not stop. They turned. Now they were running parallel to the road, on the path at the edge of the field. I ran off the driveway and through a field, hoping against logic that I could cut them off, catch up, and— what? Jump in front of them? Out of the corner of my eye I saw Mark moving like a bullet down the driveway. He'd leapt from the tractor and grabbed his bicycle, and he was tearing after the horses, leaning forward in racer position, legs like pistons, silent, fast.

My brain was electric with adrenaline, shuffling the possibilities, which ranged from bad to worse. The field ran east along the road for half a mile before turning into woods. There was a ditch between the field and the road. Would the horses hit the woods and stop? Or would they run into the ditch and wreck? Or would they turn and keep running around the farm until they hung up on something or upended? The answer was none of the above. Near the end of the field, there was a covered culvert over a ten-foot section of the ditch. Neatly, as though they'd planned it, the pair slowed slightly, made the ninety-degree turn over the culvert onto the road, and turned again, running east now on pavement, toward town.

They'd crossed the yellow line, so at least they were running in the proper lane, as they'd been trained, and not straight into oncoming traffic. I could hear them for longer than I could see them, the metal wheels of the spreader raising an enormous clatter. By the time I reached the road they were gone, out of sight over a slight hill, and so was Mark, pumping furiously behind them, gaining. Nico was on the road, too, caught up in the excitement, running crookedly on her arthritic legs, trailing the whole parade. They were a half mile from town when I last saw them. If they made it all the way, the road would end in a T, and the worst-case scenarios would get worse still.

I stood in the middle of the road and flagged down the first car that came by, driven by a middle-aged man with a beard. He was brave to stop for me, panting, hair on end, daubed with manure. He let me into the passenger seat of his car. I tried to control my breathing, told him my horses had run away, and asked if he would please drive me toward town, slowly. He asked how long it had been since they'd gotten loose, and I said I thought about fifteen minutes, which was ridiculous, in retrospect. It couldn't have been more than three. He did not comment, and I did not offer any more details. I knew the end of the story was close, and I dreaded it. The traffic was light on that road but fast. A collision was unthinkable, and Mark looked awfully vulnerable on the bicycle. I couldn't believe the horses could go at that pace much longer before one of them tripped and went down, and I couldn't force my brain to imagine what would happen after that. I do remember calculating how long it would take me to get back to the farmhouse for the gun, should one be needed.

It was a very long mile I rode with that man.

Just as we crested the small rise, I saw the horses coming toward us in the proper lane, at a calm walk, bathed in golden, late afternoon light, like the saccharine closing shot of a Hollywood movie. Mark was on the seat of the spreader, lines in his hands, smiling, and Nico was trotting along behind, tongue lolling. Neither horse looked lame, and I did not see any blood.

I rode home in the box of the spreader, and Mark told me his story. He'd caught up with the horses and pulled ahead of them on his bicycle, slowed down slightly, and told them to whoa. They had been running in the right lane, but when they saw him in front of them, they veered into the left lane. Mark inched left, and they veered back to the right. A car approached from behind them at that moment, saw what was happening, and—unbelievably—passed them on the far left. The car pulled ahead of the horses and tapped its brakes, and the horses slowed a little. Whoever was driving the car must have thought better of it then, because they sped off, leaving

Mark and the galloping horses behind. Mark struggled to stay ahead and slightly to the left of the horses, and they drifted more and more to the right until Sam, who was hitched on the right, was on the soft shoulder of the road. Mark saw with a sick feeling that they were approaching the beginning of a guardrail, a metal post strung with three strands of thick cable. In two strides they were upon it, one horse on either side. In another stride it would pass between the horses and hit the spreader, and at that speed, the spreader would flip or worse, and both horses would be maimed or killed.

That was what should have happened. What actually happened was that Sam ran on one side of the guardrail, and Silver on the other, and they both went from a dead run to a full stop in one stride, and the spreader stopped a foot before the guardrail, and both horses stood still, blowing, until Mark got to their heads. He said that when he reached for their bridles they did not look panicked as much as sheepish. He picked up the lines, took his seat, backed them away from the guardrail, then turned them around, and began the walk home.

When the rain came again it was time to put food up for winter. My neighbor Beth came over, and we canned tomatoes together, the lazy person's way, not bothering to skin or seed, just cutting them into rough chunks and throwing them in a pot to simmer overnight into a thick paste. We canned hundreds of pounds of them, the whole big wooden kitchen table covered in tomatoes and juice. At night I dreamed of tomatoes.

Mark and I bought a chest freezer, installed it in our basement, and filled it with bags of blanched chard, kale, broccoli, a lucky late planting of spinach, the last pickings of green beans and edamame. Our membership had grown to more than thirty people over the course of the season, and the fields yielded enough for everyone to store as much as they wanted.

When the freezer was full and I'd had enough of canning, we started fermenting vegetables in crocks. Freaky Sandor Katz's book *Wild Fermentation* was indispensable. Following his guidelines, I filled a five-gallon crock with a layer of garlic and dill, a few handfuls of grape leaves to add tannin, for crispness, and then a whole bushel of cucumbers, and covered everything with brine. Sandor said that was all it took. I was skeptical, but he was right. Two weeks later the pickles were ready—tangy, garlicky, alive, as good as Guss' on the Lower East Side.

Then the potatoes were ready, and they were daunting. The vines had withered on top of the rows, and underground, their tubers were big as Mark's fist, ten of them for every one we'd planted, for a total of ten thousand pounds. I was weary, and the thought of all that weight panicked me. Mark went through our phone book and called everyone we knew in the area, members and friends and acquaintances. We didn't know how many of them would come on harvest day, but any one of them would be a help.

The appointed Saturday came, and we stacked the wagon with bushel boxes, then hitched Sam and Silver to the potato digger. We'd bought it at auction, had not tested it, and weren't entirely sure it would work. It hooks to the forecart and has an adjustable prow that dips down under the hilled row, so that, as the horses pull, a thick layer of soil and the potatoes it contains flows up and over it. There is a seat where one person sits, adjusting the depth of the dig. The back of the machine is a wire belt that conveys the potatoes back to the ground, bouncing them free from dirt on the way. When it works, the digger leaves behind it a thick trail of potatoes, waiting on the surface for people to come and pick them up. Mark sat on the digger, and I drove the horses from the forecart.

We set it too deep on the first pass, and the draft was very heavy. The horses were mighty strong by the end of the season of work, and they pulled so hard that the leather tug of Silver's harness snapped, sending the evener crashing into his back legs. Mark raced back to the barn for spare harness parts while I fussed over Silver, who was aggrieved but unhurt. We fixed the harness in the field, farm-style, with a length of wire and a few wraps of electrical tape, and started again. This time we got the depth right, and the potatoes came up out of the ground like magic. Mark whooped. I stopped at the end of the row and looked back at a thick carpet of potatoes, and then I saw the cars and trucks arriving, whole families come to help. By the time we'd dug all our rows there were thirty people in the field, friends and also people I'd never met, all ages, from kids to old people, bending over buckets of potatoes, shouting and laughing between the rows. A well-organized brigade of the strongest people hauled full boxes to the wagon.

I walked the horses home and put them in their stalls and went back to the field with a pot and pints of butter. It was truly fall, the air still cold at noon despite the bright sun. The rows of popcorn had lost every trace of life, their leaves like brown paper flags rattling in the shifting breeze. We boiled potatoes in their skins in the field and served them steaming in napkins. We all warmed our chilled fingers on them, popped them open, invested them with quantities of butter and salt. If there is a more perfect way to celebrate the potato's earthy, sustaining essence, I have not yet discovered it.

The RSVPs came back from our new friends and neighbors, from old friends and family who'd be arriving from Europe, from California, from up and down the East Coast. When Mark met someone new, he issued an invitation, so the guest list had swelled to nearly three hundred. The wedding seemed like a huge wave approaching on the horizon, inexorable and possibly deadly. Still, the farm's needs trumped everything else. We listened to the weather radio for warnings of frost. The squash would need to come in before it hit or they'd be ruined, and any remaining tomatoes. Raye calved, unexpectedly. We found her big bull calf in the pasture one morning, three-quarters Holstein, lanky and spotted black and white. Raye's tricky udder swelled to twice its usual size, and milking it was like picking a lock. She was giving four gallons twice a day, and it took Mark or me two hours each milking.

One by one, I let go of the expectations I'd held for the wedding. The house would not be painted, or the cracked window fixed. The faux-brick and paneling interior would remain unapologetically faux. The lawn, at best, would be freshly grazed. At lunch we composed menus, heaped tasks on the to-do lists: Clear hay from loft, build staircase, wire for lights. Find tables and chairs. Slaughter bull for ox roast. Butcher chickens for rehearsal dinner. Write vows.

The food at harvest season is so right that the less done to it, the better. Sunday dinners were exercises in simplicity. Green salad, practically naked. Steamed green beans with butter. Beets roasted in a hot oven, sliced and tossed with a whisper of oil, a suggestion of vinegar, a bit of dill on the top. That's what we were eating when the subject of our names came up, the last Sunday before the guests arrived. I had never even considered changing my name. Nina had kept hers when she married, and so had most other women I knew. I liked my name, the alliteration of it, the solidity of its four trochaic syllables. I had nothing against his name, but this one was mine, and it stood for me, as firmly as the word *fork* stood for the thing I was holding in my hand. I didn't think I should have to give that up. I guess I'd assumed Mark knew that, even though we had not talked about it. I was shocked when he said he didn't feel the same way. He was thinking of children, and he hated the awkwardness of hyphens, and the explaining that different names entailed, especially in a community where different names are considered unusual. Besides, he said, changing your name signifies the commitment; it linguistically establishes the fact that you have become a family. Listening, I felt myself bristle, preparing to man my battle stations. "So I guess I'll take yours, then," Mark said with a shrug, a solution that seemed as simple and generous as the meal we'd made.

*   *   *

A week before the wedding, our parents arrived. All four of them did their best to hide their shock at finding hay still in the loft where the dance would be held and no preparations made beyond our to-do lists. We assigned them jobs according to their skills and interests. My mom was on cleaning, my dad was sent across the lake to Vermont, to acquire kegs of beer and hard cider. Mark's dad would build the set of stairs to the loft and wire it for lights, and his mom drew the crafty stuff, seeking out brown paper to use as table coverings, three hundred red bandannas for napkins. Mark's sister arrived with her cherubic redheaded toddler, Olin, and took charge of the flowers.

Nothing went smoothly, the consequence of no advance planning. The loft, where the dinner would be served, was splattered with pigeon manure ranging in age from ancient and powdery to fresh and wet. As my mother scrubbed the warped wood floors, the pigeons cooed from the cupola and made fresh deposits. Mark and I dashed to the hardware store and came back with chicken wire, which we used to screen out the birds. Wild birds, though, were only half the problem. Our free-range hens' coop was stationed too close to the barn, and the more adventurous among them had discovered the loft, and persisted in visiting it, to lay a sneaky egg or scratch around on the newly cleaned floor. My mother hates chickens above all living creatures. We decided we had to move the coop, both for my mother's sanity and because the guests might trip on the hens on the way up the as-yet-unbuilt stairs.

Three days before the wedding I shut the hens in the coop

when they went to roost in the evening, hooked the coop to a tractor, and hauled it fifty yards away, into the adjacent field. The next morning, the hens made their way back to the barn-yard and the loft anyway, and, worse, when evening came, they forsook the coop and roosted in their old neighborhood, a hundred of them tucked into the barnyard's hedgerow or along the rafters in the barn, above where the guests were to eat. Even we, in our muddled state, could see that this was unacceptable. Besides the tripping hazard and the mess, they couldn't sleep outside like that. They'd get eaten by owls or raccoons. We tried to corral them toward their coop with improvised nets and pieces of fence, and again and again they fluttered free. I saw my mom in her work gloves, bravely holding up one end of the net, and knew beyond any doubt how much she loved me. Eventually we abandoned the net and did it by hand, plucking all hundred hens from their roosting places, searching them out by flashlight, and chucking them, by ones and twos, into the coop, a process that took us until midnight.

Then everything was happening at once. Close friends arrived, and Mark's many cousins. Nina and her husband, David, came from California, and my brother and Dani from Virginia Beach. They all looked so foreign on the farm, in their clean civilian clothes, my sister-in-law, the pharmaceutical sales rep, wearing smart matching outfits in primary colors, unscuffed flats. Only my friend Cydni and her husband, Steve, looked at home. Cyd grew up on a ranch outside a town of forty people in Idaho, and at their wedding we bridesmaids had pulled onions from the garden for the potato salad and driven around her home valley in a pickup to collect cut flowers and eggs from the neighbors. Steve trains and shoes horses, and had grown up working drafts, so we put him in charge of the team and the wagon. Somehow, Nina got assigned to help with chicken slaughter, and I have a picture of her with a knife in one hand and a chicken foot in the other. By then she'd stopped asking the questions she'd been leaving on my answering machine for the past year—Have you resolved the chairs? Can you hire a bartender? Do you have a backup plan in case of rain?—and, as at college, had put aside her better judgment for love of me and was riding along, ready to help pick up any pieces that fell off my speeding train.

My friend Isabel arrived from London, unsure, until the last minute, if she'd be able to come. I gave her the name of a bed-and-breakfast nearby, the only one that still had rooms available. It was a grand place if you were driving by and did not slow down to look too carefully. It was owned and run by a very nice but unstable lady. When Isabel turned up, the lady had forgotten that she was coming. Isabel was the only guest, and the room she was to stay in was thick with dust and cobwebs and reeked of cigarettes. Isabel said the lady gave her a creepy Miss Havisham kind of a feeling that got much worse later that night, while she was taking a shower and the lady, apparently addled, came into the steamy bathroom calling for her mother, then sat down and used the toilet. Isabel is adventurous and loves a good story, but this was too much even for her, and we resettled her in a room adjacent to my parents' at the rental cabins down the shore.

The day before the wedding we were still hauling away the rubble from the building we tore down at the last minute, burning scraps of wood, picking up nails with a magnet. Mark's dad was hammering the last risers into the stairs he'd built to the loft. The farmhouse was filthy with tracked-in mud. There were vegetables to be harvested, washed, and chopped, the sides of beef and pork to be prepared and roasted, the tables— some acquired from a rental service, some borrowed from the church—to be set up and decorated. My mother was moving quickly, her mouth set in a thin, straight line, an expression of dread. The cartoon bubble above her head would have read "Please don't embarrass me any more than you must."

That night at the rehearsal dinner, my throat started to burn and I felt feverish. We'd picked the only restaurant open in our town in early October, a place on the lake decorated with nautical kitsch. The chef there, our friend Andy, created a meal for thirty with our ingredients: roasted young chickens, red potatoes, braised fall greens. The wine flowed freely, which helped my sore throat. Everyone raved about the food. In the next room, I could hear my friends from New York arriving. I peeked out and saw three of my ex-boyfriends together at the bar, ordering drinks. My mother gave a toast, which ended "If this is what makes my daughter happy, so be it." I was feeling dizzy with fever, and slipped out as early as I could to spend a restless night alone in a cramped and overheated room at the inn.

I wasn't entirely sure I wanted to go through with it. What if everything that my mother was saying with her facial expressions was right? What was I signing up for? Poverty, unmitigated hard work, and a man whom, for all his good points, no reasonable person would describe as easy to be with? Objectively, it wasn't exactly a good bet. There was something else, too, and I don't know why nobody talks about it. Marriage asks you to let go of a big chunk of who you were before, and that loss must be grieved. A choice for something and someone is a choice against absolutely everything else, and that's one big fat good-bye.

Our wedding day dawned moody and raw, threatening rain. Nina and David had driven south to pick up the pies we were going to serve instead of cake. Earlier in the week we'd sent south our leaf lard, for the crusts, and a load of our pumpkins, for the filling. The baker, who was doubling as the fiddler for the dance, had gotten behind in his orders, and there were no pies made, and when Nina arrived at the shop, the baker wasn't even there. It was a grand fuckup, but the kind that happens fairly regularly in North Country culture, to be expected, in the way one expects and accepts perennial lateness in Mexico, or cow-on-car accidents in Mumbai. Nina, though, was frantic on my behalf, and she and David spent most of the day speeding around the region in their rental car, buying every far-flung diner, truck stop, and roadside stand out of pies.

When I think of it now, I can see that our wedding day was exactly like our marriage, and like our farm, both exquisite and untidy, sublime and untamed. What I knew even then, though, in the middle of the chaos, was that the love at its center was not just the small human love between Mark and me. It was an expression of a larger loving-kindness, and, when I remember it, I have the feeling of being held in the hands of our friends, family, community, and whatever mysterious force made the fields yield abundant food. It is the feeling of falling, and of being gently caught.

As people arrived, they went to work, cutting flowers, chopping the vegetables, tending the barbecue with its side of beef, the hot smoker full of pork. In the loft my parents' close friends hauled bales of hay into a decorative stack, a backdrop for the fiddlers, and a makeshift aisle, strewn with flowers. They wrapped the rough rafters in strings of white lights. Someone had gone to the field and cut scores of the sunflowers, in their tall, full glory. Mark's sister has a way with flowers, and she had tied bundles of them to the loft posts. On all the tables, she'd placed Ball jars stuffed with cornflower and zinnia and purple-blue statice. The wide and dusty space looked magnificent, like a rustic cathedral. From below came the good smell of clean straw and horses, and the sound of their soft nickering, their heavy hooves.

An hour before the ceremony I was lying down in my bedroom, alone, in my dress, a cold washcloth on my feverish head. My friends Nina, Cydni, Isabel, and Brian appeared at my door. They had a bottle of Polish vodka, ice-cold from the freezer. The fiddler had not shown up in time, so I pressed Brian, a professor of French and the best singer I know, to perform an a cappella version of "Amazing Grace" at the end of the ceremony. We all took a shot, for old times, and for courage.

Mark and I were married in the barn in deference to the

rain. It was early afternoon, and the gray light pushed weakly through the dust. My sister thrust a bouquet of bloodred zinnias into my hands, and someone had brought a dog, a big, floppy Labrador who wandered among the crush of guests. We promised to take each other for richer or even poorer, and slid the gold Burmese rings onto each other's fingers. The judge pronounced us married. Mark picked me up and kissed me, and the loft erupted in applause and laughter. Brian sang "Amazing Grace," and we walked back into our crowd of friends as husband and wife.

In the wedding pictures I have a farmer's tan, dark on the face, neck, and forearms, and white on the newly muscled shoulders, the décolletage. That look pretty much spoiled the effect of the dress I'd splurged on in New York. My sister had helped me pick it out, at Dosa, a hand-stitched, gossamer thing of cotton and silk, the lightest shade of lavender gray. I'm wearing my grandmother's silk wedding shoes, from the twenties. I'm smiling maniacally, and clutching a Ball jar of hard cider; my hair, which I'd hastily plaited into two braids in a last-ditch attempt at irony, is slipping loose in pieces. Mark looks like his usual self, only cleaner, in a new white cotton shirt and gray pants, his blue sweater tied around his neck. His smile is unforced, jubilant. Next to me, his arm looped around my waist, he is so much taller than I am, we look like different species.

We recruited guests to tend the bar and pour glasses of beer and hard cider and wine. Mark's father had made a chicken-liver pâté that impressed the New York crowd, and his mom arranged slices of perfectly ripe tomatoes between basil and our farmstead cheese. There were platters stacked with sliced roast beef and barbecued pork, and loaves of fresh bread and our butter, a heaped tray of roasted root vegetables, and salads of greens and arugula. All of it we'd grown or raised. There was a whole table of Nina's pies, a spectacular collection, creams, fruits, and meringues. Friends bused dishes back and forth between the barn and the kitchen. My throat burned, I was still running a fever, and I drank too much, so the rest of the day is a blur. I do remember that the rain stopped and Mark hitched the tractor to a wagon and towed the guests around the fields, showing them the crops, the new piglets on the pasture, encouraging everyone to pick vegetables and flowers to take home. I remember the little kids from both sides—some in overalls, some in dresses—running in and out of the chicken coop with a basket full of eggs and catching the barn kittens for some forced loving. The rats were making their last stand in the older pigs' pen, in the barn, and every time someone peeped over the door the rats scattered and the people exclaimed. I remember the fiddlers finally arriving, and looking for Mark when it was time for our first dance, and not finding him, because he was downstairs in his good clothes, milking the cow.

The guests and the family cleared out slowly, and we finally collapsed into our bed, which my friends had festooned with streamers and sexually suggestive objects. The day after the wedding, the weather radio warned of a freeze, so while I coordinated the good-bye breakfast for our guests, Mark rallied a crew to harvest pumpkins. They formed a brigade, chucking pumpkins from person to person, field to wagon, and Mark got hit square in the forehead with one, and it left a set of scratches, so that, for the first week of our marriage, he looked disturbingly like Charles Manson. The frost did come that night, and the next day the sunflowers, tomatoes, the peppers and the basil and all the other tender plants were dead. What I felt was relief. No more tomatoes to pick, no more beans. Then Mark came down with the sore throat and fever, and I was still sick with it, and for several days we did not move much, only dragging ourselves out for chores and to milk Raye's bottomless udder.

We might have had a marriage of celebrity-level brevity. When everyone was gone, the presents opened and admired, the fevers broken, I had nothing left. I was empty. And I was cold. We hadn't installed our woodstove yet, and the furnace wasn't working. The guidebook publisher I'd worked for before called and offered me a last-minute gig, on Maui, and I took it. I dialed the phone with cold fingers, arranging for an apartment, a car. We'd been married a month, and I'd be gone for two. I was leaving the whole weight of the farm on Mark's shoulders, a weight that I well knew was too much even for the two of us. I told myself that it wouldn't be so bad for him, now that frost had come, and that the money from the book would make whatever he might suffer worth it. Mark joked that I was going to Hawaii for my solo honeymoon, but it was a hollow joke. I think we both knew there was a real possibility I wasn't coming back. I imagined my friends would sigh, say it was just like me, that they'd expected it all along; my parents would roll their eyes and forgive me for putting them through all that drama, and debate the proper thing to do with the wedding gifts.

At the center of my attachment to travel had always been the belief that indeed there is such a thing as escape. You can change everything with one slim ticket. The last time I'd been in the Maui airport, I'd been a girl, twenty years old, and as I walked toward my luggage, I wondered if I would find my free, young self waiting for me there among the airport greeters with their leis, or if I'd murdered her by getting married to a farmer and a farm. I supposed I would find out. Travel tends to grant clarity. Remove all that distracting context and you find yourself staring at cold hunks of truth.

There is no place on earth as far from a struggling North Country farm in November as Maui, where the warm air strokes your cheek and the fruit hangs low on the trees. I'd rented a little apartment on the ground floor of someone's very normal house, on a cul-de-sac, in a very normal subdivision in Pukalani. It was fully furnished, complete with toaster, so by the time I hung my clothes up in the closet it felt like I'd taken up a new life. That's how easy it is to leave, I thought. Nothing complex about quitting.

I commenced to do my job, which consisted of inspecting hotel rooms for island charm, tasting pupus, and trying to come up with new ways to describe white sand beaches. It was very lonely. The luaus were packed with newlyweds, faces burned pink, swaying together to the mournful sound of the slack key guitar. They looked fake to me, in their bright clothes, like extras on a set. On my restaurant rounds, I'd sit at the bar, jotting notes, and some single man would glance at my aloneness and then move away, deflected by the flash of my brand-new ring—which I'd had to cut, after all, to be resized. Maui had changed so much since the last time I'd been there. There were so many more people, and long rush hours, and not enough parking. The ocean, though, was unchanged. I walked Baldwin Beach at sunset. I rented a longboard and strapped it to the roof of my car, so I would be ready when I worked up the nerve to paddle out to the throng of people bobbing in the middle distance, waiting for the next set.

For a while I was just stunned, almost frozen, but, when I recovered from that a little, I found that what I missed first was not Mark, not the animals, but the dirt and the work. I felt, in some deep way, unnourished, like I was getting lighter, like I might just blow away.

I wandered into the health food store in the hippie surf town of Paia and searched out, in the back, a table of fresh, locally grown greens, a little pile of fruit. There was a hand-printed sign above it, with the farm's name and a phone number. I copied it down and carried it back to my apartment and dialed it, not even really knowing what I wanted. The farmer answered, and I just started talking, which is not like me. I told him about our farm, and what we grew, and the horses. I asked questions about his land, and the season, and which crops were doing well and which were not. I could tell he was busy, and I was keeping him. I felt like a lonely exile, talking to a compatriot. Just before we hung up, he said he was in a bind. His wife had left him, and they'd started this CSA thing together, just that year. He had his members to feed, and he was suddenly on his own, swamped by the work. Was there any chance I could come by to help him with harvest? He couldn't afford to pay me money, he said, but he'd send me home with some food. One could consider the parallels between his situation and Mark's, and find humor, or not.

I pulled up to his address the next morning at dawn. The mist was rising from the ground, and for a moment I thought I was in the wrong place. It looked more like a garden than a farm to me, carved out of a developed lot, surrounded by houses. A few feet away, the neighbor walked to his SUV, dressed for work in a uniform that marked him as a security guard or a cop. There was a coop of hens—a mix of white leghorns and Barred Rocks—a small grove of citrus, and a red quarter acre of rototilled clay. There was a hedge of guava, and several decorative palms. It all seemed impossibly small.

The farmer gave me a quick tour of the four miniplots that made up his vegetable operation. I could see that the problems he dealt with were different from ours. He didn't have the intense pressure of fast-growing weeds that we faced in our short growing season, but he did have a steady buildup of pests, of fungus, of various melting rots, with no cleansing, frozen break at the end of the season. No seasons, really, to speak of, only a little more wet or a little more dry. His objectives were different from ours, too. We had all the land we could possibly want, and we hedged against disasters and mistakes by planting extra and giving everything plenty of room. We had our horses for traction, which made our long rows and the sheer amount of space we kept under cultivation seem manageable. He had only this finite sliver of very expensive island, and he needed to maximize what he took from every square inch of it. His bolt-resistant lettuce mix was planted in thick patches instead of rows, in one-week successions. He did all his weeding by hand, leaning into the centers of the beds. I plucked hungrily at a leaf of peppery arugula, a sprig of spicy mustard. He handed me an orange from a tree, and I stuck my fingernail into the peel to savor its tingling smell. As dissimilar as our farms were, it was the same miracle, wrapped in different packaging. A small part of me was whispering furtively, saying, If you don't go back, you could do this, too, simple, small, get a plot, grow some food.

The farmer, though, he looked like he'd seen better days. His shorts hung on him, as though he'd recently lost weight, and he wore a badgered expression and exhaled a lot through clenched teeth. He had ten members coming to pick up vegetables that morning, he said, so we'd better get going, before the sun got too hot. He laid out coolers of ice, to chill the harvest, and two small baskets. He showed me where the collards were and told me how much he needed. I took a basket and a harvest knife and set to work.

I had been trained by Mark to work like a maniac. On our place, harvesting is not a meditation, it is a race. We take no prisoners. On his bicycle trip across the country, Mark had worked for a week with a Latino crew in New Mexico, harvesting hot peppers, and that's where he acquired his basic style. He was fascinated by their speed, and he watched carefully, to see how they did it. He saw that they worked both hands equally, favoring neither the right nor the left, always looking one step ahead, so that even before the hand dropped the pepper, it knew which one it was going to grasp next. They also sang a lot while they worked, big, lively folk songs from their home countries. So Mark became ambidextrous and learned to look ahead of his hands, and to sing those same lively songs in the field. He is the fastest worker I have ever seen. He's got preternaturally good hand-eye coordination, and that extraordinary wingspan, and his single-minded intensity. When he is really flying down a row, he looks like a living cartoon, arms and produce a peachy green blur. He collected more lessons in speed and efficiency over the years from other tutors and expanded on them, and he transmitted them all to me. After a year of harvest mornings, I could hunker down on my haunches and duckwalk along a row, my sharp knife flashing. Greens go in the bin by the armload, peas in a shower.

So that morning in Hawaii, I began harvesting the collards the only way I knew how. Not exactly at Mark-speed, but fast. My new friend, the island farmer, had started work on another item on his harvest list, but when he saw what I was doing, he was so alarmed by my pace he stopped me, arms waving, as though calling foul in a football game. It upset him so much he had to take a break and went to the house for a smoke. When he came back, calmed, he showed me how he wanted it done. His harvest style was less a death race, more of a gentle plucking. He would consider a leaf for a while. Then he would nip it off with a pair of scissors, almost reluctantly. Then he would let it flutter into the basket. It hurt me to watch him. It took the whole morning to harvest vegetables for ten people.

Watching that guy's collard flutter into his basket was the moment I got married, in my heart. There is no such thing as escape after all, only an exchange of one set of difficulties for another. It wasn't Mark or the farm or marriage I was trying to shake loose from but my own imperfect self, and even if I kept moving, she would dog me all the way around the world, forever.

I couldn't wait to get home. When I did, I dug in as deeply as I could.

Epilogue

I got back in the darkest week of winter and took up my old chores, the ones Mark had been doing for me since I'd been gone. The word *chore* connotes tedium, but that was not how I felt about them. I had missed my chores. Chores were the first taste of the weather, first effort of limbs, a dance to which I knew all the steps with certainty. Mark and I made the first few stops together, in the dark, hardly needing to speak, carrying with us the warm intimacy of our bed. We fed the two calves in the nursery pen their bottles of milk, gave them a scratch at the root of the tail, then moved to the barn, called the cows in from pasture. I fed the barn cats, and Mark spun the root grinder to chop a bushel of beets and carrots. The cows munched, we milked. I left him washing the dairy buckets and went to pour fresh water into the chickens' pans, refill their feeders with mash. Water for the dairy cows, plus a trip to the loft for four good bales of second-cut hay. By the time I rounded the west barn, on the way to the draft horses' pasture, the sun was coming up, highlighting the Green Mountains across the lake. I stopped every morning to consider the faraway, singular peak of Camels Hump. Some days it was obscured by clouds, some days tinted orange or red, and some days, when I was running early, it was visible only in two dimensions, black against a less black sky. I tried to augur the day from that view, to predict its weather and what it might hold.

When the horses and steers and pigs were all fed I walked back to the house, leaving a trail of comfort and contentment in my wake. Mark had the dairy things washed and had our own breakfast sizzling on the stove.

He'd survived my absence, but barely, and only through the help of members, friends, and neighbors. When I got back from Hawaii, something had shifted. Without me to struggle against, without the constant chaos of our first growing season, without the pressure of our impending wedding, he seemed to have found his own steady rhythm. I worked my way into it, looking for the harmony this time, instead of conflict. We found easy joy in working together, becoming real partners, instead of combatants, for the first time.

The seasons have unfolded into years. We pack them up in the fall, after frost, and label them according to the prevailing weather of the summer, by which they'll be remembered. Year two was a good one for vegetables but harder on us even than year one, and so relentlessly hot and humid that four of our Highland cows died during it. Year three was textbook perfect. Year four was somewhat dry, which stressed the plants just enough to make them exceptionally tasty. Year five was cold and disastrously wet, the dark clouds gathering over us again and again until it seemed like a joke, standing water between all the rows, three-quarters of the vegetables lost to rot. Year six it rained too much again, and late blight took all the tomatoes and the onions—three tons!—did not dry down and would not keep.

Every year the membership gets a little bigger. It hovers around a hundred now. By year three, we couldn't do it by ourselves anymore, not without risking burnout, or divorce. James and Sara and Paige came to work for us, stayed a year, then moved on to start their own farms. After that came Brad and Matt and Sam, then Susie and Anthony, and then Tim and Chad and Courtney and Racey, all young farmers aiming to gain skills that they'll use on their own places. Some of our neighbors—Kristin, Kim, Barbara, and Ronnie—joined our permanent staff. The farm has grown beyond us. On Friday nights after distribution, I cook a big dinner for everyone who worked on the farm that week, a celebration of their effort and of the harvest. In the summer the crowd runs over twenty, and we move the tables outside and send someone to the barn for extra chairs.

Our daughter, Jane, arrived in year four, at the end of that dry August. I gave birth to her in the farmhouse. Mark brought me a sunflower, and it was big as my own face and full in its moment of perfection; and when I looked at it, from the depths of the work of birth, it seemed to be looking back at me reassuringly. The midwives weighed Jane on a fish scale: seven pounds, eight ounces, a keeper. I remember waking that night with the notion in my head that the whole long trial of labor might have been a dream and there was no baby, and then finding her between us, warm and alive, and feeling not relief but almost its converse, the bright feeling of winning something unexpected at long odds. Later that week I took her to the barn to meet the horses, and held her up to Sam's big head so he could blow his breath on her, give her his blessing.

That fall we bought part of the farm from Lars, eighty acres and the house and barns.

Silver died in the winter of that same year. He and Sam had begun to show their age. The work was too much for the two of them. We'd bought another team, to take the pressure off them. Jay and Jack were Amish-bred geldings in their early teens, part Belgian, part Suffolk. I was walking back to the house after chores one cold Saturday and out of the corner of my eye I noticed Silver in the pasture, standing still, with his right foreleg cocked. It could have been a resting posture, and I almost kept going, but there was something off about him, and it made me look again. It was his expression. He looked worried. This horse was king of the pasture. He never worried. We'd turned him out with Sam and Jack after morning milking, and he'd been fine when I took hay out twenty minutes earlier. When I got to him he put his nose out and blew through his nostrils in greeting, like always. I rubbed his great, thick neck, ran my hand over his shoulder and down the leg to his knee. The leg felt sickeningly loose. He didn't flinch or pull back when I touched him. He didn't look like he was in pain, though he must have been. I knew in my heart that he was done for. I went in and told Mark, and he called the vet. Dr.

Dodd, Dr. Goldwasser's partner, was on call, and she said she would come within the hour.

When I got back out to the pasture I found Silver down, his big feet curled under him like a resting foal. The shoulder on his injured side quivered, but he was very calm. I offered him some carrots, and to my surprise he ate every one. I sat down next to him and stroked his velvet nose and tried to convey my gratitude to him for everything he'd taught me, for laboring so hard and so willingly, and for all the times that his presence had comforted me. By then I was sniveling, the tears freezing my cheeks, and my nose was running wildly. Sam walked over to us, lowered his head to touch Silver's withers, and slowly walked away. The animals, I thought, are so much more dignified in their good-byes than we humans. Dr. Dodd arrived a few minutes later. She could tell at a glance that the leg was broken above the knee. Could have been a kick from another horse, she said, or it could have been an unlucky step on a patch of ice. There was absolutely nothing that she could do for him. He stretched his neck out then and laid his head on the snow. If we had needed a sign that it was time, that would have been it. Mark walked back to the house, got the gun, and through the haze of his own tears laid the muzzle against Silver's broad forehead and put him down.

Our first Christmas as married people, Mark gave me a puppy. He was an English shepherd named Jet, black and white, a good and useful farm dog. From the beginning he was my shadow and lived to please me. The next spring Nico died, and we buried her in the yard next to the flagpole. The grass above her grave grows wilder, more rank. I think of her when I walk over it, and also whenever I look at the tuft of white fur on Jet's muzzle, the scar where Nico schooled him on not taking another dog's dinner.

We bought yet another team of horses: gorgeous young Belgians, Jake and Abby, only four years old, well-broke but without polish, a good challenge. Chad brought his own horses when he came to work for us, and in the summer our friend Bill West brings his team of Suffolks to our place every week, so there have been as many as four teams at work in the field at the same time, and anyone driving by would think we're Amish.

Sam died in the summer of year six. He had worked regularly for us until Silver died, and afterward we used him for odd jobs, or when another horse was lame. Partnered with younger horses, he was ever willing, but he tired quickly and recovered slowly. He spent his last few months with our neighbors Bob and Patti Rowe. They had a barn full of draft horses, some young and beautiful, some old relics like Sam, all of them pampered. Bob hitched Sam a few times to drag the pasture, but mostly he was retired, content to graze and doze with the rest of the Rowes' herd. Bob said that Sam took charge of the mares and their foals, acted like the herd sire, and wouldn't let the other geldings get anywhere near them. I found that surprising, because he'd always been at the bottom of the herd order on our place, under beneficent Silver while he was alive, and then under tyrannical Jack. It made me smile to hear it, like knowing your second-fiddle uncle has become the most popular guy at the nursing home. Then one bright morning Bob went out to the pasture to find all the geldings mixed in with the mares and the foals. He counted heads, and Sam was missing. Bob found him under an elm, already gone, and laid him to rest in the pasture.

Our marriage remains the fiery kind. Our front window is still cracked, the lawn is still shaggy.

It's never the way you think it'll be, Mark used to tell me. Not as perfect as you hope or as scary as you fear. A man we know bought up a big piece of good land nearby, a second home, and once, at a dinner, I heard him say, "In my retirement, I just want to be a simple farmer. I want . . . *tranquillity.*" What you really want is a garden, I thought to myself. A very, very small one. In my experience, tranquil and simple are two things farming is not. Nor is it lucrative, stable, safe, or easy. Sometimes the work is enough to make you weep. But most days I wake up grateful that I found it—tripped over it, really—and that I'm married to someone who feels the same way.

I wonder, sometimes, how Jane will regard her childhood. I am aware it's not your average one, at least not here and now. We spent her second birthday, for example, butchering rabbits. She stood on top of a barrel and watched my knife. When the rabbit was skinned and opened, she poked at a kidney with her curious first finger. "That's a kidney," I said. "It's sticky," she said. When I meet adults who grew up on farms, I quiz them on their upbringing. The answer is never lukewarm. It's either painted in golden colors—the perfect way to grow up— or described as pure drudgery, no childhood at all. The split seems to run fifty-fifty. I love this farm and the life that comes with it. I love that it makes me feel rich even though we're not. I love the work. I figure the best we can do is share that love with Jane, and hope she loves it, too.

There'd be no room for regret, if I had any. One cold winter Saturday we invited our friend Megan over for breakfast. It was her birthday, and I wanted to make something special for her. I was considering what we had in the root cellar as I walked downstairs with Jane, who was then not quite six months old. I found Mark in the kitchen, holding a calf bottle. We'd been trying to get Jane to take a bottle that week, and at first I thought Mark was making a visual joke with the gargantuan nipple, but then I saw the newborn calf in a heap at his feet. It was a bull calf, born to June and sired by Rupert. This was the third Jersey-Highland cross we'd had, and they'd all looked like Alfred E. Neuman at birth, with red, cowlicky hair and winglike ears. This one was no exception, but he was in bad shape. He must have been born right next to the electric fence and then slipped or stumbled across it, so that June couldn't get to him to lick him off. What a way to come into the world. He'd been there for a couple hours, wet, hypothermic, and he looked more dead than alive, stretched out flat on the kitchen floor.

Mark and I have developed our specialties over the years, the jobs we like best and are good at. Mark specializes in straight lines. The furrows he makes are like rulers. I specialize in doctoring the animals. My book collection contains a row of antique titles on horse and cattle husbandry, and various editions of *The Merck Veterinary Manual,* and I pore over them in the winter. So despite the breakfast to make, this calf was my project, by choice.

There's no text for cases like this, only instinct and common sense. I pried the calf's mouth open. It was cold inside. He was too far gone to suck. When I propped him up on his chest next to the woodstove, his head flopped, and amniotic fluid ran out of his nose. But where there's breath, there's hope. June's thick, warm colostrum would do him a lot of good, if we could get him warm enough to swallow it. I rubbed him vigorously with one of our good bath towels, which is the only kind of towel that is ever handy at moments like these, and stoked the woodstove. I gave him a little pep talk, telling him about the white Highland calf, his half brother, that had been born into the ice-rimmed water tank on a below-zero night in February and survived. Then I covered him with a down jacket and a bedspread and let him rest, and got back to breakfast, while Mark went to finish his chores. It would have to be a hasty meal now.

Jane was starting to fuss, so I strapped her into a baby seat and secured it on the kitchen counter and set several ladles swinging on the rack above her, which made her shriek with delight. I cracked two dozen eggs and got the pans heating on the stove. The coffeemaker was broken, and no coffee was not an option, so I boiled water and threw the grounds into it, cowboy-style. Megan arrived, and Mark and Sam and Matt came in from chores, and Jet trotted in with his girlfriend, Lady, and the two dogs licked at the calf, who was starting to look more lifelike. Lady was Jet's first assignment as a stud dog, and it wasn't going very well. She'd been with us two weeks, gradually coming into heat, and for the last four days, she'd been trying to get Jet to breed her. Jet was a jovial host but a reluctant suitor, and there'd been lots of jokes around the farmhouse about his naïveté, his preference for the barn cats, his moral rectitude, et cetera. Lady was more knowing, just waiting for his awakening.

I added more wood to the stove, and the room got toasty. The calf regained his sucking reflex, and we got a half gallon of colostrum down his gullet, which revived him enough to hold his head up. I slapped the simplified birthday breakfast—scrambled eggs with pancetta, and toast—on the table and indulged in a very big mug of coffee, a little chewy with grounds. By the time we all sat down, the woodstove was glowing faintly red and we had to move the table away from it, to the far side of the room. We'd all stripped off layers, down to the bare minimum, and still everyone was sweating. The heat did have the desired effect on the calf, though. Halfway through breakfast he popped up and frankensteined across the floor and into the next room and out again, and had to be herded away from the woodstove so he wouldn't fall into it and fry himself. He staggered into my legs while I was eating, and latched on to the bottom of the table and attempted to suck. Jane, in her infant seat, had gotten hold of a rattle, and she was shaking it and alternately giggling and happily shrieking. We were singing "Happy Birthday" to Megan when Jet finally got the hang of it, and the two dogs made their way around the table as one. It was in that sweating, giggling-shrieking, staggering, singing, doggy-style humping in flagrante chaos that I decided my life was full. Joyful, rich, but full to the brim and then some. This was not what I had pictured, when I had yearned, from my East Village apartment, for home. If I could have glimpsed it, I'm pretty sure it would have frightened me off, which is a good enough reason to be thankful for the veil of time.

And this is the place where I'm supposed to tell you what I've learned. Here's the best I can do: a bowl of beans, rest for tired bones. These things are reasonable roots for a life, not just its window dressing. They have comforted our species for all time, and for happiness' sake, they should not slip beneath our notice. Cook things, eat them with other people. If you can tire your own bones while growing the beans, so much the better for you.

In times of upheaval, I read somewhere once, people go back to the land. As economies plunged around the world, and wars droned on, on two fronts, we watched our summer volunteer staff grow and grow, filled out by high school and college students eager to learn how to plant, to weed, to harness a horse, to put up a case of tomatoes. *The New York Times* ran a trend story with the headline "Many Summer Internships Are Going Organic."

From this point I can see it was a kind of upheaval that drew me to this and to Mark. It was a grasping out of chaos, personal and general, at the cliff end of blithe youth, for something knowable. This morass, I thought then, must be a symptom of too much input. Move toward a place so small that everything could be known. If my world became a farm and a single, tiny town, I could chart and understand every person and his connections, every acre, each plant, each animal, the trajectory of each thought, emotion, and action. I wanted to believe that such a circumscribed life could be sorted and organized, in the way that the nineteenth-century naturalists cataloged all known living things, from kingdom to species, categories and subcategories that were not simple, exactly, but at least made sense.

It was, of course, nothing like that.

Megan came over the other day with her husband, Eric, to take me birding, the latest in what Mark calls my string of sudden enthusiasms. Megan and Eric were fully nerded out in buff-colored outfits, brimmed beige hats, binoculars attached to their chests with complicated-looking straps. Eric had brought his iPod stocked with recorded birdcalls, and I listened for a few minutes to the high, incomprehensible chatter. I'd begun to feel like I had some kind of bird-centered learning disability. I still couldn't tell the difference between a wren and a nuthatch. Eric, who has been watching birds for years, assured me that was normal for now.

We set out from the farmhouse, and I learned some birder lingo—MoDo for mourning dove, as in "Oh, forget it, it's only a MoDo." Flotsam for birdlike clumps of leaves. Also some birder aphorisms: *If you think it's a raven, it's a crow; if you know it's a raven, it's a raven. Let the birds come to you. If it acts like a stick, it's a stick.*

Suddenly, there were birds everywhere, birds I didn't even know existed, let alone right outside my own door. We saw an energetic, olive-colored bird in the sugar bush, a ruby-crowned kinglet, which Eric called the smallest bird with the biggest song. We heard a kind of Ping-Pong call that Eric thought might be a Nashville warbler, but the bird that was making the sound eluded us. In the acre of stunted old nursery trees, we saw a field sparrow, a species Megan had never seen before. He was at the very top of a spruce, chest puffed, head raised, wings just slightly spread, proud and theatrical like a teeny, tiny tenor. I could have watched the performance for hours. On the way back home, Eric stopped and glassed a spot in the marshy pasture just west of the house and got tense with excitement. I saw nothing until he and Megan patiently talked me to it and then, not twenty feet away, spotted a pair of savannah sparrows, a species with seventeen subspecies, and one that Eric was particularly hoping to see. I might have walked past those dull brown birds for the rest of my life and never seen them. Subcategory of a subcategory, and even the world of the sparrow is infinite.

The town is unknowable, marriage unknowable, the farm— just a single tablespoon of its soil—is a confounding mystery. But as the weeks ticked into months, into seasons, as I slowly became a farmer, something else emerged, and it was something to hold on to, something less slippery than knowing.

I've been tracking the spring peepers for seven years now. The first night they sing from the pond behind the farmhouse marks the week the fields are dry enough for work. This year, the ice and snow hung on and I thought my system would break down, but then the frozen fields yielded suddenly to a run of warm, windy days. One day there was nothing but white, and the next, there was bare black earth steaming in the sun.

Yesterday I harnessed Jay and Jack and hitched them to the spring-tine harrow, heading for the new ground that was cleared and turned last fall. The garlic to its west did not winter well. A quarter of it had not sprouted, and digging down I found the rooted clove glossy and on its way to rotten. I had a boyfriend once who liked to gamble, and I'd ride on the back of his motorcycle through the Holland Tunnel and along the New Jersey coast to Atlantic City. Sitting at the table, watching the cards being dealt, I heard a man say that the difference between an amateur and a pro is that the pro doesn't have an emotional reaction to losing anymore. It's just the other side of winning. I guess I'm a farmer now, because I'm used to loss like this, to death of all kinds, and to rot. It's just the other side of life. It is your first big horse and all he meant to you, and it is also his bones and skin breaking down in the compost pile, almost ready to be spread on the fields.

I couldn't wait to get out there, and then I couldn't wait to go in. Jay and Jack were excited by spring and their first rations of corn, from the heavy draft of the harrow over the soft, rough earth. They wanted to walk too fast, and they pushed so hard on their bits and on me that I was practically skidding over the ground, my toes jammed into the fronts of my boots. The field was full of loose, half-buried tree roots that tangled in the harrow. Every few yards I whoaed the team to lift the tines and clear them, leaving lumpy piles of dirt and rock and roots in my wake. The horses chafed at all the stopping, and then Jay antsed and backed too close to the evener, got a foot over the tug. I had to unhook and rehook it, trying not to get run over or kicked in the process, wary of the pinned ears. We got going again, and I tripped over the bight of my lines and fell flat. By now the tracks we were making in the soil were not the straight musical staff I'd been aiming for but completely abstract, slanting left, then right, interrupted by a sickle-shaped veering, the lumpy piles, and the dirt angel where I'd gone down. I rested, looked for the humor, regained my composure, and began again, and halfway down the length of the field the harrow picked up a heavy root, drew it back like a striking snake, and sent it snapping into the bone of my shin. Hot tears welled up, one-eighth pain and seven-eighths frustration. This is farming, too, just the other side of satisfaction.

By milking time the horses were lathered and blowing, and they'd remembered that they could move in a lower gear. It had been a little soon to go out after all. I'd pugged up the low patches and muddied the horses' bellies. Another few days, though, and the great crescendo of spring would begin, the list of things to do fast outpacing the things that can be done. At least we'd set back the quack grass and pulled up some of those dreadful roots.

Unknown outpaces known like to do outpaces done. These acres are a world. What answers has the ground offered? Only the notion that there are answers. Underlying soil is bedrock, and if you dig deep enough, you'll hit it. That's the closest I've come to surety, and it is enough for me.

Acknowledgments

Huge thanks to my friend, former boss, and agent, Flip Brophy at Sterling Lord Literistic, who never saw this book coming when she hired me to answer the phone. Thanks to Sharon Skettini and Judy Heiblum, who helped see it through. At Scribner, thank you to Nan Graham, Kara Watson, and Paul Whitlatch for their skill and support.

I could not have written this without the help of friends and family. Thanks especially to David and Margie Reuther, who are responsible for getting the book started, and also for helping me finish up at the end. Nina Nowak and Peter Lindberg were first readers and steadfast supporters, and David Schairer provided generous amounts of technical help. Thank you to Ronnie and Don Hollingsworth, Barbara Kunzi, and Beth Schiller for being such good friends to us and loving caregivers to Jane, and to everyone at the Essex Volunteer Fire

Department, where much of the book was written. Thanks to Lars and Marit Kulleseid, for giving us a chance to farm this good land. Thank you to my parents, Tony and Linda Kimball, for a lifetime of support, and for hosting Jane and me for long stretches in the book's final stages. Thank you to my sister, Kelly Kimball, for absolutely everything. And all my love and thanks to Mark and Jane, who have patiently waited.